Contents

Features

The *Practical Science* series will help children succeed in science. Science concepts are presented through engaging, easy-to-implement experiments using materials readily available at home, school, or local stores. After completing the series, children will be armed with the concepts and confidence they need to achieve at a higher level in science class and on standardized tests.

Practical Science: Standards-Based Experiments, Grades 3–4 contains 3 units: Physical Science, Life Science, and Earth Science. Each unit is divided into 4 lessons. The content of all 12 lessons is based upon National Science Education Standards (NSES) and the Full Option Science System (FOSS) Modules for Grades 3–4.

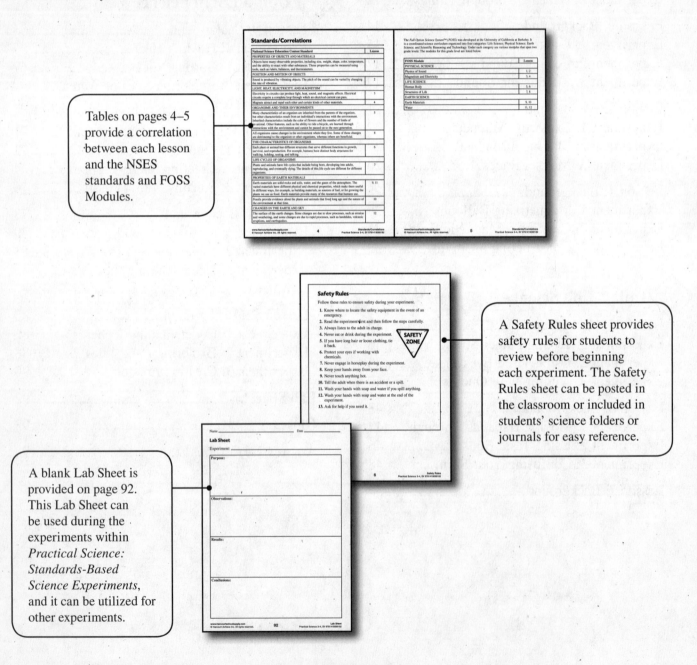

Tables on pages 4–5 provide a correlation between each lesson and the NSES standards and FOSS Modules.

A Safety Rules sheet provides safety rules for students to review before beginning each experiment. The Safety Rules sheet can be posted in the classroom or included in students' science folders or journals for easy reference.

A blank Lab Sheet is provided on page 92. This Lab Sheet can be used during the experiments within *Practical Science: Standards-Based Science Experiments*, and it can be utilized for other experiments.

Practical Science 3–4, SV 9781419099182

The Lessons begin on page 7. Each lesson consists of a Background page followed by 3 experiments. While the lessons are written for the student, it is advised that the teacher or parent walk the student through the background and experiments to ensure understanding.

The Background provides a summary of the main concepts covered in the lesson. It includes key vocabulary words in boldface, which are fully defined in the Glossary on pages 93–94.

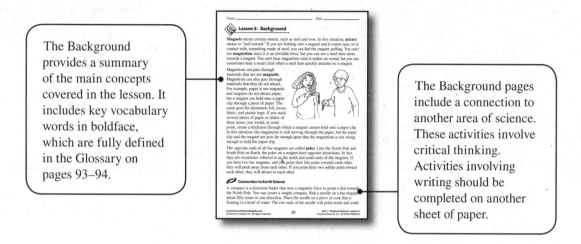

The Background pages include a connection to another area of science. These activities involve critical thinking. Activities involving writing should be completed on another sheet of paper.

A Materials list details all required materials. Room is given so that students can place a check mark by each item.

Each Experiment begins with a Purpose. This explains the focus of the experiment and what will be done.

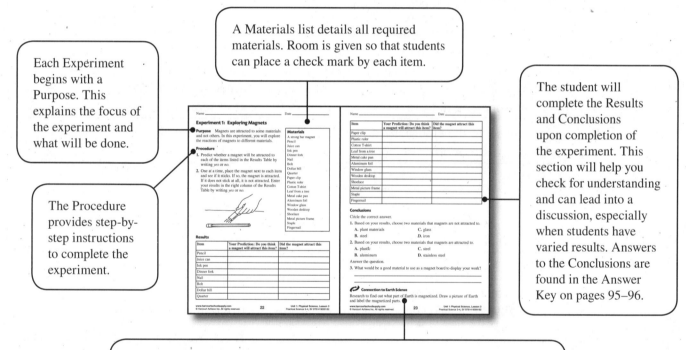

The student will complete the Results and Conclusions upon completion of the experiment. This section will help you check for understanding and can lead into a discussion, especially when students have varied results. Answers to the Conclusions are found in the Answer Key on pages 95–96.

The Procedure provides step-by-step instructions to complete the experiment.

Most experiments include a Connection to another area of science. As in the Background, these activities help students think critically about the science topic. Activities involving writing should be completed on another sheet of paper.

The experiments presented in this book can be used to introduce, review, or extend science concepts. In addition, they may also be used as a basis for a more in-depth project, such as for a science fair. In this case, the student should locate additional information about the topic from books or the Internet.

Science is about discovery and exploration. The experiments in *Practical Science: Standards-Based Science Experiments* provide students with ample opportunity to discover and explore scientific concepts. Through this process, science will become exciting and interesting.

Standards/Correlations

National Science Education Content Standard	Lesson
PROPERTIES OF OBJECTS AND MATERIALS	
Objects have many observable properties, including size, weight, shape, color, temperature, and the ability to react with other substances. Those properties can be measured using tools, such as rulers, balances, and thermometers.	1
POSITION AND MOTION OF OBJECTS	
Sound is produced by vibrating objects. The pitch of the sound can be varied by changing the rate of vibration.	2
LIGHT, HEAT, ELECTRICITY, AND MAGNETISM	
Electricity in circuits can produce light, heat, sound, and magnetic effects. Electrical circuits require a complete loop through which an electrical current can pass.	3
Magnets attract and repel each other and certain kinds of other materials.	4
ORGANISMS AND THEIR ENVIRONMENTS	
Many characteristics of an organism are inherited from the parents of the organism, but other characteristics result from an individual's interactions with the environment. Inherited characteristics include the color of flowers and the number of limbs of an animal. Other features, such as the ability to ride a bicycle, are learned through interactions with the environment and cannot be passed on to the next generation.	5
All organisms cause changes in the environment where they live. Some of these changes are detrimental to the organism or other organisms, whereas others are beneficial.	8
THE CHARACTERISTICS OF ORGANISMS	
Each plant or animal has different structures that serve different functions in growth, survival, and reproduction. For example, humans have distinct body structures for walking, holding, seeing, and talking.	6
LIFE CYCLES OF ORGANISMS	
Plants and animals have life cycles that include being born, developing into adults, reproducing, and eventually dying. The details of this life cycle are different for different organisms.	7
PROPERTIES OF EARTH MATERIALS	
Earth materials are solid rocks and soils, water, and the gases of the atmosphere. The varied materials have different physical and chemical properties, which make them useful in different ways, for example, as building materials, as sources of fuel, or for growing the plants we use as food. Earth materials provide many of the resources that humans use.	9, 11
Fossils provide evidence about the plants and animals that lived long ago and the nature of the environment at that time.	10
CHANGES IN THE EARTH AND SKY	
The surface of the earth changes. Some changes are due to slow processes, such as erosion and weathering, and some changes are due to rapid processes, such as landslides, volcanic eruptions, and earthquakes.	12

www.harcourtschoolsupply.com
© Harcourt Achieve Inc. All rights reserved.
4
Practical Science 3–4, SV 9781419099182

The *Full Option Science System™ (FOSS)* was developed at the University of California at Berkeley. It is a coordinated science curriculum organized into four categories: Life Science; Physical Science; Earth Science; and Scientific Reasoning and Technology. Under each category are various modules that span two grade levels. The modules for this grade level are listed below.

FOSS Module	Lesson
PHYSICAL SCIENCE	
Physics of Sound	1, 2
Magnetism and Electricity	3, 4
LIFE SCIENCE	
Human Body	5, 6
Structures of Life	7, 8
EARTH SCIENCE	
Earth Materials	9, 10
Water	11, 12

Practical Science 3–4, SV 9781419099182

Safety Rules

Follow these rules to ensure safety during your experiment.

1. Know where to locate the safety equipment in the event of an emergency.

2. Read the experiment first and then follow the steps carefully.

3. Always listen to the adult in charge.

4. Never eat or drink during the experiment.

5. If you have long hair or loose clothing, tie it back.

6. Protect your eyes if working with chemicals.

7. Never engage in horseplay during the experiment.

8. Keep your hands away from your face.

9. Never touch anything hot.

10. Tell the adult when there is an accident or a spill.

11. Wash your hands with soap and water if you spill anything.

12. Wash your hands with soap and water at the end of the experiment.

13. Ask for help if you need it.

Practical Science 3–4, SV 9781419099182

Name _____ Date _____

Lesson 1: Background

The human ear has three main parts: outer, middle, and inner. The job of the **outer ear** is to gather sound. As **sound waves** enter the outer ear, they are squeezed together when they hit the **eardrum**. The **vibrations** are sent from the eardrum to three tiny bones in the **middle ear**. The middle ear moves the sound waves into the **inner ear**. Within the inner ear, the sound waves create **nerve impulses** that travel to the brain. These nerve impulses are what a person really hears when a sound is made. Although there are a lot of steps involved, the steps happen so fast that it is only a small time between when a sound wave is captured by the outer ear and the brain hears the sound.

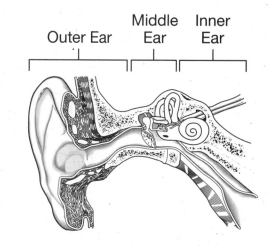

Outer Ear   Middle Ear   Inner Ear

Many times, people can recognize sounds without seeing where the sound came from. For example, you can probably recognize some people's voices on the telephone without actually seeing the people. But sometimes, if you hear an unexpected sound, you might not be sure what it is. For example, if it is a bright sunny day, and you think you hear thunder, you will probably look around to see what is causing the noise.

Sound waves travel through the air, but they also travel through other materials. Some materials are good **conductors** of sound, while others are not. The speed of sound differs for each material. The closer the **molecules** are in a material, the easier the sound will be heard. Scientists and manufacturers have worked together to use the differences in how materials react to sound waves to create both **soundproofing** and **sound amplification**. The **force** of sound waves against the ears is measured in **decibels**. We use decibels to measure loudness. Even without knowing the decibel level of a noise, you can decide for yourself if a sound is loud or soft.

 Connection to Earth Science

Make a list of sounds that occur naturally and could be confused with thunder.

Experiment 1: Knowing What You Hear

Purpose   You can usually hear a sound and tell what it is, even when you can't see the sound being made. In this experiment, you will test your ability to identify sounds you cannot see.

Procedure

1. Take a turn going behind the carrel, curtain, or poster board to make a noise as directed by the adult.

2. When not making a noise, identify the noises you hear and describe them in the Results Table.

3. After each noise is made and you are finished writing your description, put your pencil down and look at the adult so he or she knows to tell the noisemaker to reveal how the noise was made.

4. In the table, circle *yes* or *no* to tell if you were right about the noise.

5. If you make one of the noises, draw a wavy line through that row in the Results Table.

Materials

Adult helper

Carrel, curtain, or standing poster board on desk or tabletop

Sheet of aluminum foil to crinkle

Stapler and a sheet of paper to staple

Sports whistle to blow

Fork to tap on a glass container

Marbles to roll around in a glass container

Sandpaper to rub on a brick

2 teaspoons to clink together

2 plastic mixing spoons to beat together

2 wooden cutting boards to bang together

Large rubber band stretched over a box so the rubber band can be snapped

Knuckles to rap on a tabletop

Dishtowel to snap in the air

Textbook with pages to fan through

Plastic bag to blow up and pop

Results

Noisemaker	Identification/Description	Were you correct?	
1		yes	no
2		yes	no
3		yes	no
4		yes	no

Name _____ Date _____

Noisemaker	Identification/Description	Were you correct?	
5		yes	no
6		yes	no
7		yes	no
8		yes	no
9		yes	no
10		yes	no
11		yes	no
12		yes	no
13		yes	no
14		yes	no
15		yes	no

Conclusions

Answer the questions.

1. Would you have been better able to recognize what was making each noise if you had seen all the noisemakers before the experiment? Why?

_____

_____

2. Which two things made similar noises?

_____

_____

3. Which noisemaker was the most difficult to identify? Why?

_____

_____

Connection to Life Science

Make a list of at least five noises you might hear in nature. Explain why you would or would not be able to identify each sound without seeing it being made.

Name _____ Date _____

Experiment 2: Identifying Loud and Soft

Purpose Vibrations make sounds. The larger the vibration, the louder the sound will be. In this experiment, you will predict the loudness and softness of five noises and then you will check your predictions.

Materials
Plastic ruler
Textbook (about 2 inches thick)
Empty large-sized tissue box
Carpet pad on a desktop
2 inch × 4 inch board (about 6 inches long)
Empty plastic container

Procedure

1. Think about firmly tapping the textbook, tissue box, carpet pad, board, and plastic container with the plastic ruler.

2. Look at the two middle columns of the Results Table and think about how the five different items will rank when tapped.

3. In the first column of the Results Table, predict and write the ranking of the five items.

4. Firmly tap each of the five items with the plastic ruler. Try to tap each item with the same force.

5. In the last column of the Results Table, rank the items based on the actual noise each made. Complete the column. Repeat tapping the five items as needed to make your decisions.

Results

Prediction (Your Guess) About Ranking	Loud/Soft Ranking	Sound Wave Vibration Ranking	Actual Ranking
	Loudest	Largest	
	Second loudest	Second largest	
	Middle	Middle	
	Second softest	Second smallest	
	Softest	Smallest	

Name _____ Date _____

Conclusions

Answer the questions.

1. Did your predictions match the actual results? Explain.

_____

_____

2. Imagine you have a clubhouse and you want to cover the walls to soundproof them. Based on your results, what is a material you would suggest for covering the walls? Explain.

_____

_____

_____

3. Does sound travel better through some materials than others? Explain.

_____

_____

_____

↻ Connection to Earth Science

Think about hearing the natural Earth sounds of thunder, running water, and wind blowing. For each, note a situation where people would hear the sound the loudest and a situation where people would hear the sound the most quietly.

Name _____ Date _____

Experiment 3: Hearing Through Things

Purpose Sound travels through some materials better than others. In this experiment, you will explore how well sound travels through different materials.

Procedure

1. Set the timer for 1 hour so that it will tick continuously through the experiment.

2. In the second column of the Results Table, predict whether, through each of the items, you will hear the ticking the same as without the item at your ear, whether the item will block some of the ticking, or if the item will block the ticking completely. Circle your prediction.

3. One at a time, pick up each item. Listen to the ticking with both ears. Then use your right hand to cover your right ear and hold the item to your left ear. (If you are unable to cover both ears, have a partner help you.)

4. Listen for the level of ticking you hear.

5. Circle the actual result for each item in the last column of the Results Table.

Materials

Timer with an audible ticking sound

2-inch-thick book

Wooden cutting board, about 1-inch-thick

Metal cake pan with a metal lid or a cookie sheet to hold over the pan as a lid

Full box of cereal

Throw pillow

Plastic food container with a plastic lid

Zipper plastic bag full of water (make sure it does not leak)

Balloon blown up to about a 15-inch diameter

Results

Items	Predictions	Actual Results
Book	Blocks none	Blocks none
	Blocks some	Blocks some
	Blocks all	Blocks all
Wooden cutting board	Blocks none	Blocks none
	Blocks some	Blocks some
	Blocks all	Blocks all

Name _____ Date _____

Items	Predictions	Actual Results
Metal cake pan	Blocks none Blocks some Blocks all	Blocks none Blocks some Blocks all
Cereal	Blocks none Blocks some Blocks all	Blocks none Blocks some Blocks all
Pillow	Blocks none Blocks some Blocks all	Blocks none Blocks some Blocks all
Plastic container	Blocks none Blocks some Blocks all	Blocks none Blocks some Blocks all
Bag of water	Blocks none Blocks some Blocks all	Blocks none Blocks some Blocks all
Balloon	Blocks none Blocks some Blocks all	Blocks none Blocks some Blocks all
Hand	Blocks none Blocks some Blocks all	Blocks none Blocks some Blocks all

Conclusions

Answer the questions.

1. Did your predictions match the actual results? Explain.

_____

_____

2. Which of the materials blocked the most sound? _____

3. Which of the materials blocked the least sound? _____

 **Connection to Earth Science**

Use a zipper bag full of dirt to conduct one more of the sound experiments above. Then read to find out about what people hear at the beginning of earthquakes.

Lesson 2: Background

Whenever anything makes a sound, it vibrates. These vibrations bump into **air molecules**, which cause the air molecules to bounce around and bump into other air molecules, which bump into other air molecules. This chain reaction results in sound waves. When you hear a sound, it is the result of sound waves that are reaching your ears. Although sound vibrations are mainly connected with hearing, we can also see and feel sound vibrations. Sound waves travel through air as well as **solids** and **liquids**. Different materials have different effects on sound vibrations.

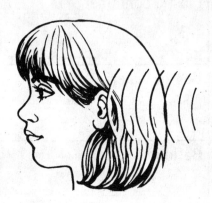

When you hum, talk, or sing, your vocal cords vibrate in your throat. You can feel this vibration through your throat simply by placing your hand on the outside of your throat. The louder the noise you make with your voice, the stronger the vibration you will feel on the outside of your throat. Many solids, such as bone and wood, carry sound waves much better than air, so the resulting sound is louder. This knowledge is the basis for hearing aids that transfer sound waves directly to the bone behind the ear. This movement of sound waves, sending sounds from the bone directly to the inner ear, is called **bone conduction**. People with little or no hearing through their ears are usually able to hear through the bone.

 Connection to Life Science

Look in books, magazines, encyclopedias, or on the Internet to find at least one animal that appears to naturally use bone conduction to hear.

Name _____ Date _____

Experiment 1: Looking at Sound

Purpose   Although we do not usually think about seeing sound, we can see sound waves if we try hard enough. In this experiment, you will arrange to "see" some sound waves.

Materials
8- or 9-inch diameter bowl
Clinging plastic wrap
1 tablespoon of rice
Hard plastic stirring spoon
Metal cookie sheet
Inch ruler

Procedure

1. Firmly stretch the plastic wrap over the bowl until it creates a wrinkle-free tight covering with at least 1 inch left over on the side.

2. Gently spread the rice over the bowl covering.

3. Look closely at the rice. Notice the placement of the rice on the plastic wrap. Record your observations in item 1 of the Results.

4. Hold the cookie sheet upside down in the air about 1 inch from the bowl. Do not touch the bowl, the plastic, or the rice.

5. With the spoon, bang on the backside of the cookie sheet so that the noise is directed at the rice. Bang on the cookie sheet for about 15 seconds.

6. While you are banging on the cookie sheet with the spoon, observe the rice. Record your observations in item 2 of the Results.

7. After you are finished banging on the cookie sheet, put it down and look at the rice. Record your observations in item 3 of the Results.

8. Repeat the procedure, beginning about 1 inch from the bowl and slowly moving away until the rice stops moving.

9. While you hold the cookie sheet in place, have a partner measure the distance from the bowl. Record your observations in item 4 of the Results.

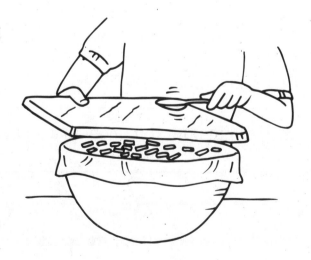

Name _____ Date _____

Results

Follow the directions.

1. Describe what the rice looks like.

_____

_____

2. Describe the appearance of the rice as you bang on the pan the first time.

_____

_____

3. Describe the appearance of the rice after you stop banging on the pan the first time.

_____

_____

4. Tell how far away the pan is from the bowl when the rice stops moving the second time you bang on the cookie sheet.

_____

Conclusions

Follow the directions.

1. Explain how you know some of the sound waves from the noise you made reached your ears.

_____

_____

2. Explain how you know some of the sound waves went in the direction of the rice.

_____

_____

3. Explain how you know that sound waves weaken as they travel.

_____

_____

⟳ Connection to Life Science

Try moving the rice without using props. Can you send out a strong enough sound wave that you can see or hear?

Experiment 2: Feeling Sound

Purpose Sometimes you can feel sound vibrations. In this experiment, you will feel sound in several situations.

<table>
<tr><td>

Materials

For every 2 or 3 students:

Sports whistle

TV or radio

Sheet of paper rolled and taped into a megaphone shape

One-hour timer

Musical instrument

</td></tr>
</table>

Procedure

1. Holding your head and neck as still as possible, place your hand on the front of your neck and hum.

2. Continue humming and holding still while you move your hand to your lips. Record what you feel in the Results Table.

3. Have one member of your group blow the whistle. As the whistle sounds, touch your finger along the side of it. Record what you feel in the Results Table.

4. Turn on the TV or radio and place your hand on the speaker. Record what you feel in the Results Table.

5. Have one member of your group talk into the homemade megaphone while you hold your hand on the outside of it. Record what you feel in the Results Table.

6. Turn the timer on so that it begins ticking and place your hand on it. Record what you feel in the Results Table.

7. Have one member of your group play the musical instrument while you hold your hand on the outside of it. Record what you feel in the Results Table.

Results

Sound maker	What, if anything, did you feel?
Humming	
Whistle	

Sound maker	What, if anything, did you feel?
TV or radio	
Voice in megaphone	
One-hour timer	
Musical instrument	

Conclusions

Answer the questions.

1. What can the volume of a sound tell you about what is making the sound vibrations?

_____

_____

2. If you were to remove one sound maker from this experiment, which would it be and why?

_____

_____

3. How were the noises different when you made a noise and tried to feel the noise vibrations at the same time?

_____

_____

4. Which sound maker made the softest sound in the experiment?

_____

_____

Connection to Life Science

Research to find information about wild animals that react to sound vibrations.

Name _____ Date _____

Experiment 3: Conducting Sound

Purpose   Most sound vibrations reach the ear through air. But, in some situations, vibrations travel though solids, such as wood and bone. In this experiment, you will experience the difference between air and solid sound conduction.

Materials
Partner
4 carrot sticks
Yardstick
Timer
Countertop or tabletop

Procedure

1. Working with a partner, chew two carrot sticks each. Use your hands to cover your ears and listen to your own chewing. Then with your ears uncovered, listen carefully to your partner's chewing.

2. Circle the option that sounded the loudest to you in row 1 in the Results Table.

3. Hold a yardstick at waist level, tap on the yardstick, and listen to the sound. Hold the yardstick to one ear and use one hand to cover the other ear. Reach a foot or so down the yardstick, tap with your fingernail, and listen to the sound.

4. Circle the option that sounded the loudest to you in row 2 in the Results Table.

5. Turn a timer on so that it ticks. Note how the timer sounds. Hold a yardstick so that it touches the ticking timer and your ear. Use one hand to cover your other ear and then note how the timer sounds.

6. Circle the option that sounded the loudest to you in row 3 in the Results Table.

7. Tap your fingernail on the counter or tabletop and note how the tapping sounds. Rest an ear on the counter, use one hand to cover the other ear, and tap again. Note how the tapping sounds now.

8. Circle the option that sounded the loudest to you in row 4 in the Results Table.

Results

	Pair	Choice 1	Choice 2
1	2 people chewing carrots	You chewing carrots	Your partner chewing carrots
2	2 yardstick tappings	Tapping at waist level	Tapping with yardstick at ear
3	2 timer tickings	Ticking through air	Ticking through yardstick
4	2 counter tappings	Tapping through air	Tapping through counter

Conclusions

Answer the questions.

1. Did any of your results surprise you? Explain.

_____

_____

_____

2. Is sound conducted better through the air or through a solid? Explain.

_____

_____

_____

 Connection to Earth Science

You are sitting in a treehouse halfway up a tree and a friend is sitting farther away from the tree on a blanket. Which one of you is likely to hear the sounds of nature, such as crickets chirping or birds singing, more loudly? Explain.

Name _____ Date _____

Lesson 3: Background

Magnets attract certain metals, such as steel and iron. In this situation, **attract** means to "pull toward." If you are holding onto a magnet and it comes near, or in contact with, something made of steel, you can feel the magnet pulling. You can't see **magnetism** since it is an invisible force, but you can see a steel item move towards a magnet. You can't hear magnetism since it makes no sound, but you can sometimes hear a small click when a steel item quickly attaches to a magnet.

Magnetism can pass through materials that are not **magnetic**. Magnetism can also pass through materials that they do not attract. For example, paper is not magnetic and magnets do not attract paper, but a magnet can hold onto a paper clip through a piece of paper. The same goes for aluminum foil, tissue, fabric, and plastic bags. If you stack several sheets of paper or others of these items, you would, at some

point, create a thickness through which a magnet cannot hold onto a paper clip. In this situation, the magnetism is still moving through the paper, but the paper clip and the magnet are now far enough apart that the magnetism is not strong enough to hold the paper clip.

The opposite ends of all bar magnets are called **poles**. Like the North Pole and South Pole on Earth, the poles on a magnet have opposite attractions. In fact, they are sometimes referred to as the north and south ends of the magnets. If you have two bar magnets, and you point their like poles towards each other, they will push away from each other. If you point their two unlike poles toward each other, they will attract to each other.

 Connection to Earth Science

A compass is a direction finder that uses a magnetic force to point a dial towards the North Pole. You can create a simple compass. Rub a needle on a bar magnet about fifty times in one direction. Place the needle on a piece of cork that is floating in a bowl of water. The two ends of the needle will point north and south.

Name _____ Date _____

Experiment 1: Exploring Magnets

Purpose Magnets are attracted to some materials and not others. In this experiment, you will explore the reactions of magnets to different materials.

Procedure

1. Predict whether a magnet will be attracted to each of the items listed in the Results Table by writing *yes* or *no*.

2. One at a time, place the magnet next to each item and see if it sticks. If so, the magnet is attracted. If it does not stick at all, it is not attracted. Enter your results in the right column of the Results Table by writing *yes* or *no*.

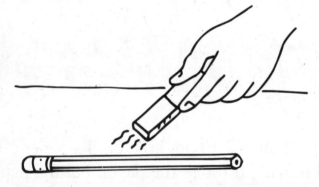

Materials

A strong bar magnet
Pencil
Juice can
Ink pen
Dinner fork
Nail
Bolt
Dollar bill
Quarter
Paper clip
Plastic ruler
Cotton T-shirt
Leaf from a tree
Metal cake pan
Aluminum foil
Window glass
Wooden desktop
Shoelace
Metal picture frame
Staple
Fingernail

Results

Item	Your Prediction: Do you think a magnet will attract this item?	Did the magnet attract this item?
Pencil		
Juice can		
Ink pen		
Dinner fork		
Nail		
Bolt		
Dollar bill		
Quarter		

Name _____ Date _____

Item	Your Prediction: Do you think a magnet will attract this item?	Did the magnet attract this item?
Paper clip		
Plastic ruler		
Cotton T-shirt		
Leaf from a tree		
Metal cake pan		
Aluminum foil		
Window glass		
Wooden desktop		
Shoelace		
Metal picture frame		
Staple		
Fingernail		

Conclusions

Circle the correct answer.

1. Based on your results, choose two materials that magnets are not attracted to.

   A. plant materials   **C.** glass

   B. steel   **D.** iron

2. Based on your results, choose two materials that magnets are attracted to.

   A. plastic   **C.** steel

   B. aluminum   **D.** stainless steel

Answer the question.

3. What would be a good material to use as a magnet board to display your work?

_____

_____

↻ Connection to Earth Science

Research to find out what part of Earth is magnetized. Draw a picture of Earth and label the magnetized parts.

Name _____ Date _____

Experiment 2: Making a Magnet

Purpose Permanent magnets are always magnets and are always attracted to steel. Some items can become temporary magnets that are attracted to steel for a short amount of time. In this experiment, you will turn a paper clip into a temporary magnet.

Materials

For each set of partners:

5 small metal paper clips (each about 1 inch long)

Table space

Large metal paper clip (almost 2 inches long)

Strong bar magnet

Procedure

1. Place the small paper clips on a table.

2. Using the large paper clip, touch the small paper clips to see if they are attracted. Complete row 1 in the Results Table.

3. Place the large paper clip on the magnet so the paper clip sticks out over the edge about 1 inch.

4. Holding onto the magnet and with the paper clip pointing downward, try to pick up a small paper clip. Complete row 2 in the Results Table.

5. Next try to pick up as many of the small paper clips as you can. Complete row 3 in the Results Table.

6. Return the small paper clips to the tabletop. Take the large paper clip, hold it about 10 inches off the table, and drop it onto the table.

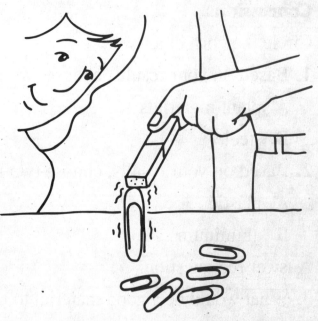

7. Pick up the large paper clip and hold it up to the small paper clips to see if they are now attracted. Complete row 4 in the Results Table.

8. Hold one end of the large paper clip in your hand. Moving in only one direction, rub the other end of the paper clip across the magnet 50 times.

9. Touch the large paper clip to a small paper clip to see if they are now attracted. Complete row 5 in the Results Table.

10. Using the large paper clip, pick up as many small paper clips as you can. Complete row 6 in the Results Table.

Name _____ Date _____

Results

1	Are the paper clips naturally attracted to each other? How do you know?	
2	Would you say that the paper clips are attracted now? How do you know?	
3	How many paper clips were you able to pick up? Once you picked one up, was it easy to hold onto it while you picked up another?	
4	After dropping the large paper clip onto the table, is it still attracted to the other paper clips? How do you know?	
5	Does the large paper clip attract to the small paper clip? How do you know? Explain.	
6	How many small paper clips were you able to pick up? Was it as easy as picking up the small paper clips with the large paper clip attached to the magnet?	

Conclusions

Answer the questions.

1. Are paper clips magnetically charged most of the time? Explain how you know.

_____

_____

2. Why is the large magnet considered to be a temporary magnet?

_____

_____

Circle the correct answer.

3. When you compare the rubbed paper clip to the paper clip attached to the magnet, you can see that the rubbed paper clip—

A. is not really a magnet.   **C.** is able to hold the charge longer.

B. is a weaker magnet.   **D.** is dangerous.

 Connection to Earth Science

Look to find naturally occurring materials that attract to magnets.

Name _____ Date _____

Experiment 3: Magnet Races

Purpose You already know that a magnet attracts a paper clip. The purpose of this experiment is to find out if a magnet can attract a paper clip through a piece of paper.

Materials

For every 3-person team:

Bar magnet

Small paper clip

Copy of page 27

Procedure

1. Place the paper clip on the magnet to make sure it attracts to the paper clip.

Two team members:

2. Hold page 27 horizontally and as level as possible.

Third team member:

3. Remove the paper clip from the magnet and place it on the star at the corner of the page.

4. Holding the bar magnet under the paper, move it around until you find the paper clip and can move it with the magnet.

5. Move the paper clip along the path as quickly as possible.

6. If the paper clip gets completely off the track, start back over at the star.

7. Keep track of the number of times you have to start over.

Results

1. How many times did your team have to start over? _____

2. Did your team make it all the way around the track? _____

Conclusions

Answer the questions.

1. Did you have any problems controlling the paper clip? Explain.

_____

_____

2. What did you learn about the ability of a magnet to attract through paper? Explain.

_____

_____

Name _____ Date _____

 Connection to Life Science

Explore to see if magnets are attracted to parts of living things. Use a bar
magnet and items such as a feather, some fur, a deer horn, an eggshell, a leaf,
a pine cone, a carrot, and a banana peel.

Name _____ Date _____

Lesson 4: Background

Have you ever walked across carpet, touched someone, and felt a shock? When you walked across the carpet, you built up **static electricity**. When you touched the other person, an electrical spark jumped from you to the other person.

This balloon shows a typical, neutrally charged balloon with matching positive and negative charges.

You can also create static electricity using a balloon. A balloon typically has a neutral **charge**. If you rub a balloon on a rug, piece of clothing, or your hair, the rubbing creates **friction**. The friction gives the balloon a negative charge and, for example, the hair, a positive charge. Since opposite charges attract, the balloon and the hair are attracted to each other and the balloon will stick to the hair. If the balloon is pulled from the hair, the positively charged hairs will **repel** from each other, causing each strand to stand straight up.

To understand electricity, you must understand magnetism, because the two are closely related. Many modern electrical and electronic products rely on magnetism. Computers, video cameras, speakers, electric motors, hair dryers, telephones, vacuum cleaners, and generators all use magnets. There are three types of magnets:

- **Permanent magnets**
- **Temporary magnets**
- **Electromagnets**

You worked with permanent and temporary magnets in Lesson 3. In this lesson, you will explore batteries and **electric currents** as you create a **circuit**. An electric current is made when charges move from place to place. All parts of the circuit must be joined to work. A circuit that works is called a closed circuit. If any part is not joined, it is an open circuit. Electrical energy created by an electrical circuit is part of an electromagnet.

 Connection to Life Science

Look in books, magazines, encyclopedias, or on the Internet to find the effect electricity has on humans, other animals, and plants.

Experiment 1: Magnetizing Balloons

Purpose   One kind of electricity is called static electricity. People can easily create static electricity, and you will create it in this experiment.

Materials

Balloon that blows up to about a
   10-inch diameter
Partner
Paper towel
Desk or table
$\frac{1}{4}$ cup uncooked rice

Procedure

1. Blow up the balloon and tie it so the air stays in.

2. Take the balloon and rub it on your partner's head until his or her hair stands up or to the count of twenty. Record the results in row 1 of the Results Table.

3. Touch the balloon against your partner's shirt and then quickly let the balloon go. Record the results in row 2 of the Results Table.

4. Do not touch the balloon after it is placed on the shirt.

5. Place the paper towel flat on the desk or table.

6. Put the uncooked rice on top of the paper towel.

7. Take the balloon and rub it on your shirt while you slowly count to 20.

8. Lower the balloon towards the pile of rice. Get within $\frac{1}{8}$ inch of the rice, but do not touch the rice. Record your observations in rows 3 and 4 of the Results Table.

Results

1	How did your partner's hair look after it was rubbed?	
2	What happened when the balloon was placed against your partner's shirt, but not held there?	
3	Where was the balloon when the rice was being put on the paper towels?	
4	Describe what happened as the balloon was lowered towards rice on a paper towel.	

Conclusions

Answer the questions.

1. What are two quick ways to create static electricity?

_____

_____

2. Think about the balloon that was used in the experiment. How long did the static electricity last?

_____

_____

_____

3. Static electricity in the balloon causes it to react like—

   A. water.

   B. magnets.

   C. deflated balloons.

   D. heavy items.

4. Which of the following is another example of static electricity?

   A. Apples shrivel when they get old.

   B. Window shades move when the windows are open.

   C. Clothes from the dryer stick together.

   D. Water runs down the driveway when the hose is left on.

 Connection to Life Science

Describe a possible situation where you could create static electricity with the help of an animal.

Name _____ Date _____

Experiment 2: Creating a Magnetic Field

Purpose A magnetic force field is usually invisible. In this experiment, you will look at a magnetic force field that you use a magnet to create.

Materials
$\frac{1}{2}$ cup steel or iron shavings or filings
Gallon-sized zipper bag
Bar magnet
2 sheets of paper
Magnifying glass

Procedure

1. Place the steel or iron shavings or filings in the zipper bag.

2. Place the bar magnet flat on a table.

3. Place the two sheets of drawing paper over the magnet.

4. Place the bag of steel or iron on top of the drawing paper.

5. Lightly pound on the table near the drawing paper.

6. Watch the magnetic field appear.

7. Use the magnifying glass to more closely look at the steel or iron pieces.

Results

In the box below, make a drawing showing the shape of the force field. Very lightly, in the center of your drawing, outline the shape of the bar magnet.

Name _____ Date _____

Conclusions

Answer the question.

1. The bar magnet is rectangular. What is the shape of the magnetic field that it creates?

_____

Circle the correct answer.

2. The steel or iron shavings or filings gather at the points where the magnet is the strongest. Which part(s) of the bar magnet is the strongest?

    A. the middle

    B. one of the ends

    C. both of the ends

    D. no area appears stronger than any other

3. Which part(s) of the bar magnet has the weakest magnetism?

    A. the middle

    B. one of the ends

    C. both of the ends

    D. no part appears weaker than any other

4. Why do you think the experiment procedures include lightly pounding near the drawing paper?

    A. It is actually the pounding that produces the magnetic field.

    B. It helps to speed up the process and evenly spread out the metal.

    C. Table vibrations help to magnetize the bar magnet.

    D. The pounding determines where the strongest part of the magnet will form.

Connection to Earth Science

Look in books, magazines, encyclopedias, or on the Internet to find out why Earth is referred to as a giant magnet.

Experiment 3: Constructing a Circuit

Purpose   When a battery is connected properly, electric current flows through a circuit or path. In this experiment, you will create an electric circuit using a lemon as the battery.

Procedure

1. Squeeze the lemon and roll it on the table to loosen the inner juices.

2. Have an adult helper use the sharp knife to cut two $\frac{1}{2}$-inch slices in the lemon. Have the helper place the slices about $\frac{1}{2}$ inch apart.

3. Slide the dime halfway into one of the slices.

4. Slide the penny halfway into the other slice.

5. Gently touch your tongue and lips to the dime and penny at the same time.

6. Pay close attention to what you feel as you touch the coins.

7. Take the coins out and wash them.

8. Throw the lemon away.

Materials
Lemon
Adult helper
Sharp knife
Dime, washed and dried
Penny (older than 1982 so that it contains copper), washed and dried
Soap

Results

Answer the question.

Describe what you felt when your tongue touched the coins.

_____

_____

_____

Conclusions

Answer the questions.

1. What type of circuit do the lemons, coins, and tongue represent when they are not joined?

   _____

2. What type of circuit do the lemons, coins, and tongue represent when they are joined?

   _____

3. During the experiment, what was occurring as you touched the coins with your tongue?

   _____

   _____

4. Would you have felt anything if you had only touched one of the coins? Explain.

   _____

   _____

   _____

 Connection to Earth Science

Explain how lightning can become part of a closed electric circuit.

Lesson 5: Background

The human body has about 650 **muscles**. Each of the different muscles has a job to do. Some of the muscles are much longer and stronger than others. In this lesson, you will explore some of the muscles of the human hand.

It is easy to confuse human eyes, or at least to make the eyes seem like they are fooled. These "eye tricks" are called **optical illusions**. Here are some interesting eye tricks.

When eyes stare at a bright image for a period of time, the eyes become tired. Tired eyes then might recreate the image where it doesn't actually exist and in different colors. Such an "eye error" lasts only a few seconds.

Look at the two sets of circles on the right. The middle circles in each set are the same size. The eyes will see two same-size circles as different sizes when tiny circles surround one of the circles and large circles surround the other circle.

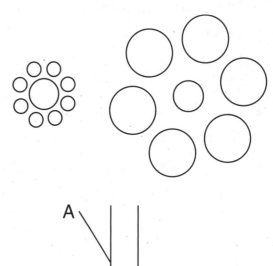

 In a drawing such as the faces/ vase on the left, the eyes can switch back and forth between looking at the background and looking at the foreground.

The diagonal line layout shown on the right can confuse the eye as to which of the two lines on the right align with the single line on the left. You can use a ruler or a sheet of paper to check for sure.

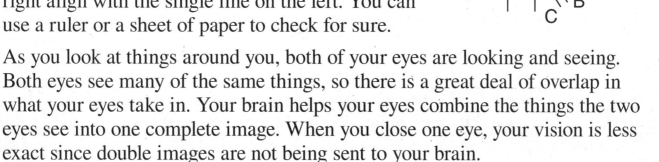

As you look at things around you, both of your eyes are looking and seeing. Both eyes see many of the same things, so there is a great deal of overlap in what your eyes take in. Your brain helps your eyes combine the things the two eyes see into one complete image. When you close one eye, your vision is less exact since double images are not being sent to your brain.

 Connection to Earth Science

Research desert **mirages**. Explain what part of a mirage is an eye trick and what part is due to the desert's appearance.

Name _____ Date _____

Experiment 1: Testing Finger Strength

Purpose   Each muscle in the human body has a set purpose and capability. In this experiment, you will test the ability of the finger muscles to push backwards.

Materials
3 toothpicks per student
Inch ruler
Desk
Partner

Procedure

1. Place one toothpick under your middle finger and over your ring and index fingers as shown.

2. Have your partner measure 1 foot above the top of the desk.

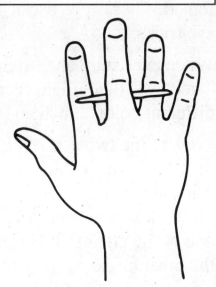

3. Place your hand in the air at the 1-foot mark and push with your fingers in an effort to break the toothpick. Push as hard as you can while your partner counts to 10.

4. Try one more time. Record your results in the Results Table.

5. With the toothpick still in place, rest your hand on the desktop with your palm down.

6. Push as hard as you can to try to break the toothpick while your partner counts to 10.

7. Try one more time. Write your results in the Results Table.

8. Ask five other students, including your partner, how they did in their efforts to break the toothpicks. Write the other students' names at the top of the last five columns. Record the other students' responses in the Results Table.

Results

	Did the toothpick break? (Write *yes* or *no* for each trial for each person.)					
	You					
first in air						
second in air						

Name _____ Date _____

Did the toothpick break? (Write *yes* or *no* for each trial for each person.)						
first on desktop						
second on desktop						

Conclusions

Circle the correct answer.

1. Based on your results, which of these statements sounds accurate?

   A. The muscles in the hand and middle finger are not able to push backwards with much force.

   B. The muscles in the hand and index finger are not able to push forwards with much force.

   C. The muscles in the hand and ring finger are not able to push at all.

   D. None of the three fingers have muscles with pushing power.

Answer the questions.

2. Does the desk provide the necessary force for the index finger, the middle finger, or the ring finger to hold itself while the other two fingers break the toothpick?

   _____

3. Were you able to break the toothpick in the air? _____

 Connection to Physical Science

Explore how wedges, levers, and pulleys work. Then explain which, if any, of these have limitations such as the finger muscles have.

Name _____   Date _____

Experiment 2: Using Tired Eyes

Purpose Human eyes make mistakes when they get tired. In this experiment, you will explore mistakes of the eyes.

<table>
<tr><td>Materials
Copy of this page
Red marker
Yellow marker
Sheet of white paper
Partner
Timer</td></tr>
</table>

Procedure

1. Using the markers and staying within the lines, completely color the stars in the rectangles below. Color the left star red and the right star yellow. Do not leave any white streaks showing through.

2. Pick up the white sheet of paper and stare at it while your partner counts to 25.

3. In the Results Table, record any colors and shapes you see.

4. Place the white paper where you can quickly pick it up later.

5. Have a partner set the timer for 1 minute.

6. For 1 minute, stare at the white space between the two star rectangles.

7. When the timer rings, look quickly from this paper to the white paper. Stare at the white paper while your partner slowly counts to 20.

8. In the Results Table, record any colors and shapes you see.

Results

What color(s) and shape(s) do you see when you first look at the white paper? If you do not see any, write *none*.	Draw the color(s) and shape(s) you see when you look at the white paper after looking at the space between the red- and yellow-star boxes. If you do not see any, write *none*. (If you do not remember the colors, repeat the experiment.)

Conclusions

Answer the questions.

1. Did the image you see move around? Explain what it did.

_____

_____

2. In what color did your tired eyes recreate the black? _____

3. In what color did your tired eyes recreate the red? _____

4. In what color did your tired eyes recreate the yellow? _____

↻ Connection to Earth Science

Explain how this experiment might relate to astronomers who study the moon and the stars in the night sky.

Name _____ Date _____

Experiment 3: Aiming with One Eye

Purpose   Most people see with two eyes. In this experiment, you will explore seeing with just your left eye and just your right eye.

Materials
Partner
Tape
Copy of page 42
Fine-tip markers: blue, black, and red

Procedure

1. Have your partner assist you in taping page 42 to the wall to use as a target.

2. Have your partner assist you in standing back from the target so that, with your writing arm stretched straight in front of you and a capped marker in your hand, you can just touch the circle in the middle of the page.

3. Have your partner hand you uncapped markers as needed for Steps 4–7.

4. With both eyes open and using the black marker (uncapped), pull your arm back to your head and then quickly spring your arm forward, aiming at the center of the circle. Make sure that your marker touches the paper so that you leave a mark showing where you touched.

5. Repeat Step 4 four more times so you have five black marks on your target.

6. With only your right eye open, and using the red marker, aim five times.

7. With only your left eye open, and using the blue marker, aim five times.

Results

As shown in the sample finished target, connect your five black marks, your five red marks, and your five blue marks.

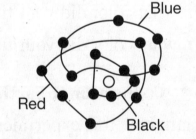

Sample finished target

Conclusions

Answer the question.

1. Based on your results, is your left eye or your right eye most like your vision with two eyes? Explain how you know.

_____

_____

Name _____ Date _____

Circle the correct answer.

2. Based on your results, which statement is the MOST correct?

   A. My best aim is with my two eyes together.

   B. My best aim is with my left eye only.

   C. My best aim is with my right eye only.

   D. I do not have very good aim with either eye.

3. Based on your results, which statements are correct?

   A. My five trials with my left eye only (blue) are all about equal distance from the center of the circle.

   B. My five trials with my right eye only (red) are all about equal distance from the center of the circle.

   C. My five trials with both eyes (black) are all about equal distance from the center of the circle.

   D. None of my trial sets had points that were about equal distance from the center of the circle.

Answer the question.

4. Think about looking through a telescope like the boy in the picture is doing. Which eye would you use? Why?

_____

_____

 Connection to Physical Science

Research the safety of a person driving if he or she has been injured and has a patch on one eye.

Name _____ Date _____

Lesson 6: Background

The human body is made up of 11 systems. In this lesson, you will explore parts of two body systems: the digestive system and the integumentary system.

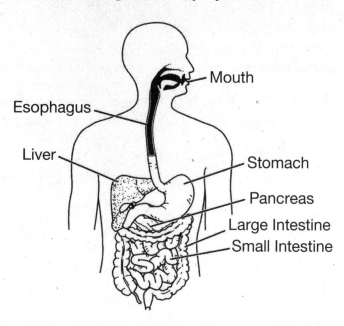

The **digestive system** is a group of organs that processes food. The body breaks down food to use.

The digestive process begins when you put food into your mouth. **Saliva** joins the food as you chew it to make it small enough to swallow. The food then goes into your stomach, through the **small intestines**, and into the **large intestines** before leaving the body. Along the way, food is broken down so the body can use it. While food is in the small intestine, the body absorbs the **nutrients** the body can use. The remaining food parts go on to the large intestine and prepare to leave the body. The small and large intestines **contract**, or decrease and grow in size, to move the food along.

Taste buds are also part of the digestive system. The diagram shows areas of taste on the tongue. However, any level of flowing saliva within the mouth can confuse exact taste bud locations since food particles easily move around with saliva.

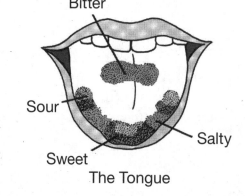

The Tongue

The **integumentary system** includes the outer covering of the human body. It includes skin, hair, nails, and **sweat glands**. One of the functions of skin is to help maintain body temperature. Your skin can adjust to the temperature of the area around you. Your skin allows you to adjust to cold temperatures when you dive into a cold lake. It also lets you step into a hot shower or a hot tub and adjust to the temperature.

 Connection to Earth Science

Explain how the sun and human skin do and do not work together.

Name _____ Date _____

Experiment 1: Moving Bananas Through

Purpose   Digestion is the process of breaking food down so the body can use it. In this experiment, you will act out a part of the digestion process.

Materials

Pair of pantyhose with the toe seams cut out

Overripe banana

Cake pan

$\frac{1}{2}$ cup water

Procedure

1. Tie a knot in the waist of the pantyhose. Place the knot so that smashed banana can pass under the knot from one leg of the pantyhose to the other.

2. Place the cake pan where you can put something through the pantyhose and have it end up in the cake pan.

3. Peel the banana, put the banana pulp into the pantyhose, and throw the peeling away.

4. Use your fingers to work the banana through the pantyhose and out the other end.

5. Add a little bit of water and keep working the banana through.

6. In the Results Table, describe how you worked the banana through the pantyhose and the appearance of the banana as it comes out of the pantyhose.

Results

Describe how you worked the banana pulp through the pantyhose.	Describe what the banana pulp looked like as it came out of the pantyhose.	Describe how your hands looked after you finished.

Conclusions

Answer the questions.

1. Were you surprised by any of the results of this experiment? Explain.

_____

_____

_____

2. How does this experiment relate to the digestive system?

_____

_____

_____

Circle the correct answer.

3. In this experiment, the banana pulp on your hands represents—

    A. a realistic eating experience.

    B. food that does not taste good.

    C. fiber that the body needs.

    D. nutrients that are absorbed by the body.

 Connection to Physical Science

Use bananas and the pantyhose again to prove that gravity helps with digestion and to learn if gravity needs help to move food through the digestive system.

Name _____ Date _____

Experiment 2: Using Taste Buds

Purpose Different areas of the human tongue are associated with different taste sensations. In this experiment, you will locate these different areas on your own tongue.

Materials

For each student:

6-slot cupcake pan

1 tablespoon water combined with 1 tablespoon salt

1 tablespoon water combined with 1 tablespoon sugar

1 tablespoon water combined with 1 tablespoon coffee

1 tablespoon lemon juice

4 small stick-on labels

Marker

4 cotton swabs

Mouth-rinsing collection can (such as a 1-gallon can)

3 glasses of water for rinsing mouth

Paper towel

Procedure

1. Place each of the four mixtures in one of the cupcake slots.

2. Use the marker and the stick-on labels to identify each of the four mixtures.

3. Place a cotton swab in each cupcake slot.

4. Rinse your mouth by taking a sip of water, swishing it around, and spitting it out into the rinse collection can.

5. Stick your tongue out of your mouth a little so that you can reach different parts of it with a cotton swab.

6. Choose one of the four solutions and, one at a time, touch each of the following areas of your tongue. Try to keep your tongue out of your mouth and away from your saliva. Rinse your mouth between each area of your tongue that you test.

   • tip of your tongue by your front six teeth

   • front side of your tongue

   • back side of your tongue

   • center back of your tongue

7. As you touch the different areas of your tongue, decide where the taste is strongest and mark it in the Results Table. Write *strongest* in the appropriate boxes. Leave the rest of the boxes empty.

8. Repeat Steps 4–6 with the other three solutions. Use the paper towel to dry your mouth as needed.

Name _____ Date _____

Results

	Tip	Front Side	Back Side	Center Back
Sugar Water (sweet)				
Salt Water (salty)				
Lemon Juice (sour)				
Coffee (bitter)				

Conclusions

Follow the directions.

1. Next to the areas of the tongue where you tasted them most strongly, write the names of the solutions you tried.

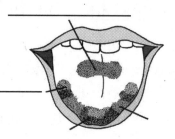

Answer the questions.

2. Did you experience any confusion as you tried to make strong-taste-area choices? Explain.

_____

_____

3. Does licking an ice-cream cone work well with the taste areas of the tongue? Explain.

_____

_____

4. Some people who drink coffee direct a drink past the tip of the tongue to the center-back of the tongue. Others direct the coffee more to the front of the tongue. Based on your results, which group of people do you think probably most like the strong taste of coffee? Explain.

_____

_____

 Connection to Earth Science

With the help of an adult, find minerals that have a bitter taste.

Practical Science 3–4, SV 9781419099182

Experiment 3: Confusing Your Skin

Purpose   As a rule, you can touch something and have a good idea how warm or cold it is. In this experiment, you will see that your skin can be fooled about temperature.

Procedure

1. At the same time, place one hand in the hot water and one hand in the ice water.

2. Keep your hands inside the bowls for 2 minutes.

3. Remove both hands and place them in the bowl with room temperature water for about 10 seconds. Notice how your hands feel.

4. Use a paper towel to dry your hands.

Materials

Bowl of hot tap water (not so hot that you can't touch it)

Bowl of ice water

Bowl of room temperature water

Clock or watch that shows minutes and seconds

Paper towels

Results

Follow the directions.

1. Describe how your hand that was in the hot water felt when you put it in the room temperature water.

   _____

   _____

2. Describe how your hand that was in the ice water felt when you put it in the room temperature water.

   _____

   _____

Conclusions

Answer the questions.

1. Did the room temperature water feel the same to both hands? Explain.

   _____

   _____

2. How might this experiment have been different if you had only put your hands in the ice water and hot water for 10 seconds?

_____

_____

_____

Circle the correct answer.

3. Which of the following statements BEST describes what happened when you put your hands in the room temperature water?

   A. The two sides of the bowl of room temperature water were at different temperatures.

   B. The cold hand is warming up, and the hot hand is cooling down. You sense the feeling of hot or cold depending on the direction heat is flowing from each hand.

   C. The cold hand is warming up the hot hand, and the hot hand is warming up the cold hand. The room temperature water goes along with this warming and cooling.

   D. Both hands are actually warming up even though they do not both necessarily feel that way.

4. By leaving your hands in the ice water and hot water for 2 minutes, you gave your hands a chance to—

   A. reject the water temperatures.

   B. adapt to the water temperatures.

Connection to Earth Science

Explain how this experiment relates to the steam that comes off a lake after the sun goes down.

Name _____ Date _____

Lesson 7: Background

Structures of life include all parts of plants and animals and how they function. Understanding how plants and animals begin life is one key piece of information that will help you understand life in general.

Most plants grow with roots underground, so you cannot watch them grow. Since some hardy seeds can grow on a wet paper towel instead of underground, it is possible to watch roots grow. As you watch roots grow, you will see a lot of growth some days and less other days. You will also see that no matter how a seed is positioned, the roots will grow downwards and the plant will grow upwards.

Plants need food to grow, and most plants begin with a seed and make their own food from air, water, and sunlight. Even the largest tree started out as a small seed.

Human beings are **omnivores**, which means that they eat both plants and animals. So, it is not surprising that you will find many plants, seeds, and roots at a supermarket. Here is a list of some items that you can find in a grocery store that you can plant and expect to grow:

Seeds of any fruit
Potatoes
Dried beans
Dried peas
Nuts that have been neither roasted nor salted
Bird feed
Onion
Sunflower seeds that have been neither roasted nor salted
Organic wild rice

Scientists have been studying plants and animals for centuries. Some early beliefs are no longer viewed as likely. For example, the Greek philosopher, Aristotle, believed that **maggots** grew from rotting flesh. Since Aristotle was well regarded as an educated man, many other scientists agreed with his viewpoint. Today we know that a new life, such as a maggot, cannot develop from a non-living item such as a piece of rotting meat. In addition, we now know that maggots are actually the offspring of flies and that maggots hatch from fly eggs.

↻ Connection to Physical Science

Explain what roots have to do with balance. Look to find out how roots grow to balance some specific different-sized plants from a small flower to a large tree.

Name _____ Date _____

Experiment 1: Growing Plants Without Dirt

Purpose   Since most plant roots grow underground, you do not see the roots. In this experiment, you will plant a seed in a clear plastic glass so you can watch the roots grow.

Procedure

1. Have the adult helper use the letter opener to create a $\frac{1}{2}$-inch diameter (approximately) watering hole in the center bottom of the glass.

2. Wet the paper towel so that it is thoroughly damp, but not dripping.

3. Crumple the paper towel and stuff it in the glass.

4. Place the three bean seeds between the paper towel and the side of the glass.

5. Use the black marker to write *A*, *B*, and *C* above the beans.

6. Set two pencils parallel about 1 inch apart on a paper plate.

7. Turn the glass with the paper towel and beans in it upside down and place it on the pencils.

8. Use the eyedropper every day to add 1 whole eyedropper of water through the watering hole.

9. For a period of 2 weeks, use the ruler and the Results Table to keep track of the changes you see in the seed and to measure the growth that takes place daily.

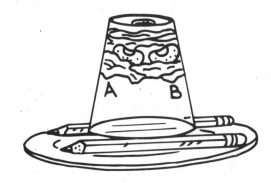

Results

Week One		Mon.	Tues.	Wed.	Thurs.	Fri.
Seed A	Appearance					
	Plant (mm)					
	Root (mm)					

Week One		Mon.	Tues.	Wed.	Thurs.	Fri.
Seed B	Appearance					
	Plant (mm)					
	Root (mm)					
Seed C	Appearance					
	Plant (mm)					
	Root (mm)					

Week Two		Mon.	Tues.	Wed.	Thurs.	Fri.
Seed A	Appearance					
	Plant (mm)					
	Root (mm)					
Seed B	Appearance					
	Plant (mm)					
	Root (mm)					
Seed C	Appearance					
	Plant (mm)					
	Root (mm)					

Conclusions

Answer the questions.

1. For how many days was the seed "planted" before it started to grow? _____

2. Did the seed grow a root or a stem first? _____

3. How did light affect the plant's growth?

_____

_____

 Connection to Earth Science

In an effort to understand how a wet paper towel can replace soil, make a list of the similarities between soil and a wet paper towel.

Name _____ Date _____

Experiment 2: Planting Groceries

Purpose   Many grocery items that we eat as food can also be planted and grow into a plant. In this experiment, you will explore some of these different items.

Materials

Internet access

From each student: a different seed that is found in a grocery store and can be planted

Note: Assign seeds to students in advance to prevent duplications.

Procedure

1. Search the Internet to find directions for planting the grocery item you have chosen.

2. Observe the plants' growth for 2 weeks.

3. Use the Results Table to keep track of the different types of plants that the class planted and when each plant first showed growth.

Results

Student: **Planted:** **Show Date:**	**Student:** **Planted:** **Show Date:**	**Student:** **Planted:** **Show Date:**
Student: **Planted:** **Show Date:**	**Student:** **Planted:** **Show Date:**	**Student:** **Planted:** **Show Date:**
Student: **Planted:** **Show Date:**	**Student:** **Planted:** **Show Date:**	**Student:** **Planted:** **Show Date:**
Student: **Planted:** **Show Date:**	**Student:** **Planted:** **Show Date:**	**Student:** **Planted:** **Show Date:**
Student: **Planted:** **Show Date:**	**Student:** **Planted:** **Show Date:**	**Student:** **Planted:** **Show Date:**
Student: **Planted:** **Show Date:**	**Student:** **Planted:** **Show Date:**	**Student:** **Planted:** **Show Date:**

Name _____ Date _____

Student:	Student:	Student:
Planted:	Planted:	Planted:
Show Date:	Show Date:	Show Date:
Student:	Student:	Student:
Planted:	Planted:	Planted:
Show Date:	Show Date:	Show Date:
Student:	Student:	Student:
Planted:	Planted:	Planted:
Show Date:	Show Date:	Show Date:

Conclusions

Answer the questions.

1. Did any of the items have planting instructions that surprised you? Explain.

_____

_____

2. Did the larger seeds or the smaller seeds sprout first? Give examples.

_____

_____

3. Did seeds or non-seeds grow first? Give examples.

_____

_____

4. Were the plants that sprouted first the tallest plants when the last plant finally sprouted? Give examples.

_____

_____

Connection to Earth Science

Do you think students in different climates could all perform this experiment at the same time? Explain why or why not.

Practical Science 3–4, SV 9781419099182

Name _____   Date _____

Experiment 3: Watching Meat Spoil

Purpose Meat spoils in different ways depending upon the circumstances. In this experiment, you will explore three slightly different settings for spoiling meat.

Materials

3 jars

$3\frac{1}{4}$-inch slices of cooked turkey

6-inch diameter paper circle

2 pieces of cheesecloth,
   4 inch × 4 inch

2 rubber bands that easily
   stretch to a 3-inch diameter

wire pet cage large enough to
   hold 3 jars

Procedure

1. Choose a time of year when the low temperature is 60°F or higher.

2. Place one slice of turkey in each of the three jars.

3. Use a rubber band to secure the paper circle over one of the jar openings.

4. Use a rubber band to secure two layers of cheesecloth over one of the jar openings.

5. Leave the third jar open.

6. Place all five jars in the pet cage.

7. Place the pet cage outside and securely fasten the cage to keep the jars safe.

8. Check on the jars daily for 10 days and record any changes in the Results Table. Describe how the meat looks and smells.

Results

	Paper-covered jar	Cloth-covered jar	Open jar
Day 1			
Day 2			
Day 3			
Day 4			
Day 5			
Day 6			
Day 7			
Day 8			
Day 9			
Day 10			

Conclusions

Answer the questions.

1. How long did it take for maggots to appear? _____

2. Did the meat smell bad before the maggots appeared? _____

3. Maggots come from the hatching of fly eggs. What does this fact have to do with the results?

   _____

   _____

   _____

4. Will meat spoil with and without maggots? Explain.

   _____

   _____

   _____

5. In this experiment, why was it important to put the jars in a cage?

   _____

   _____

   _____

Connection to Earth Science

Even though the jars in this experiment are in a cage, how might natural forces of Earth still ruin the experiment?

56

Name _____ Date _____

Lesson 8: Background

All **organisms** cause changes in their **environments**. Although you can rarely see what plant roots are doing underground, they are very busy breaking up dirt, clinging to dirt, and holding dirt in place in heavy rains. When large areas of land are not covered with plants, the land is much more likely to be washed away in hard rains. **Soil erosion** refers to land that is carried away by water. Farmers plan carefully to avoid soil erosion.

Farmers can help prevent soil erosion through sound farming practices such as crop rotation, strip cropping, and leaving crop residue on a field. **Crop rotation** means "to change which crops are planted in which fields." For example, if corn is  planted in a field for two years, then alfalfa or soybeans could be planted next. **Strip cropping** refers to planting a few yards of one crop and then a few yards of another crop. Combining crops in this way helps make sure that crops with a poor grip on the soil do not allow erosion. Leaving **crop residue** refers to leaving some plant pieces in a field so that rain and wind do not reach the dirt. Modern-day harvesting equipment makes it easy to cut crops so that residue, such as corn stalks and corn stalk leaves, remains on the ground.

People other than farmers also make changes to the soil environment without realizing it. Spilling a half can of soda on the grass seems like a harmless act. However, you have just watered grass with something other than water. Do you know how grass reacts to soda? You see a pretty wildflower, and you snip off the flower. Will this action cause the wildflower to grow more or less flowers than it was going to grow? Every interaction you have with nature can change the environment.

Other living things change the environment, too. For example, think about how the environment changes when a tree root grows into a drainpipe, or dandelions start growing all over a yard. Nonliving things can also change the environment. A huge storm can form, or a boulder can roll off a cliff. Every environment on Earth changes in many ways every day.

 Connection to Earth Science

Research to make a list of at least five long-lasting environmental changes that are a result of natural events on Earth.

Practical Science 3–4, SV 9781419099182

Name _____ Date _____

Experiment 1: Holding Soil

Purpose   Plant roots intertwine in soil as a way to hold a plant upright. This intertwining also helps prevent soil erosion. In this experiment, you will explore how roots hold onto soil.

Materials
Newspaper Table An established potted plant that has at least 10 inches of growth and that has not been watered for 2 days

Procedure

1. Spread the newspaper out on the table to create a workspace.

2. Place your hand around the plant next to the soil.

3. Turn the plant upside down.

4. Shake the pot and pull gently on the plant until the plant and dirt come out of the pot. Keep holding the plant.

5. Look at the shape of the dirt. Circle the BEST response in box 1 in the Results Table.

6. Shake the plant gently while you count to 20.

7. Look at the roots. Circle the BEST response in box 2 in the Results Table.

8. Shake the plant firmly while you count to 20 again.

9. Look at the roots. Circle the BEST response in box 3 in the Results Table.

Results

1 Coming out of the pot, the dirt is—	2 The roots—	3 The roots—
a. shaped like the pot. b. in a crumbled pile on the newspaper. c. partially hanging on the roots and partially scattered on the newspaper.	a. have no dirt left on them. b. fell with the dirt onto the newspaper. c. hung onto quite a bit of dirt.	a. have no dirt left on them. b. still have quite a bit of dirt clinging to them. c. are quite broken and damaged.

Conclusions

Answer the questions.

1. How would the results be different if this experiment were done with a newly planted plant? Explain.

_____

_____

_____

2. Based on your results, during which times are farmers' fields more and less safe from erosion? Describe those times.

_____

_____

_____

Circle the correct answer.

3. Roots have a natural tendency to—

   A. cling to the soil in which they are growing.

   B. ruin the soil in which they are growing.

   C. harden the soil in which they are growing.

4. Based on your results, it is logical to say that plant roots are—

   A. always green.

   B. unimportant.

   C. flexible.

 Connection to Earth Science

Look in books, magazines, encyclopedias, or on the Internet to find out how trees and their roots grow differently in rich soil versus in rocky soil.

Experiment 2: Digging a Tunnel

Purpose   Even a small amount of digging in Earth changes the environment of the soil in that area. In this experiment, you will see firsthand some of the things that digging in the soil can change.

<table>
<tr><td>Materials
Garden gloves or other type of glove
  to cover hands
Adult helper
Spade
About 8 square feet of land to dig
5-gallon bucket of water</td></tr>
</table>

Procedure

1. Put on the garden gloves.

2. Use a spade to dig two holes that are about 1 foot deep and 2 feet apart. Have the adult help you as needed.

3. Dig a tunnel between the two holes.

4. Study everything that came out of the holes and everything that you can see in the holes. Then complete the first three columns of the Results Table.

5. Pour the bucket of water into your holes.

6. Fill in the fourth column in the Results Table.

7. Pack the dirt back into your tunnel and holes.

Results

• With #4 • Number of plants uprooted or chopped through	• With #4 • Number of creatures you can see in the dirt piles	• With #4 • Number of rocks moved out of the holes	• With #6 • What happened to the water that went into your holes?

60

Name _____ Date _____

Conclusions

Answer the questions.

1. At the conclusion of this experiment, how was the ground different than when you first found it?

   _____

   _____

   _____

2. Did this experiment affect any living things? Explain.

   _____

   _____

   _____

3. Did this experiment affect any nonliving things? Explain.

   _____

   _____

   _____

4. How will the water affect the soil?

   _____

   _____

   _____

Connection to Earth Science

Look in books, magazines, encyclopedias, or on the Internet to find out how soil is different in rainy climates versus dry climates.

Name _____ Date _____

Experiment 3: Changing the Environment by Walking

Purpose You likely cause changes in the environment every day without realizing it. In this experiment, you are going to use heightened awareness to focus on environmental changes you are making.

<table>
<tr><td colspan="2">Materials</td></tr>
</table>

Materials

Adult helper

A sunny day

A forest or other tree-covered area
   to walk

First-aid kit

For each student:

Hiking clothes

Pencil

Notebook or clipboard to use as a
   writing surface during walk

Procedure

1. Although most walks in a forest do not result in anyone being injured, make sure the adult helper has a first-aid kit and is prepared to handle emergencies.

2. Take a 10-minute nature walk on a sunny day. Avoid walking on an existing path. Try not to change the environment as you walk.

3. Walk single file with each person looking for environmental changes caused by the person in front of him or her.

4. Each time you see the person in front of you change a natural part of the forest, such as a plant, animal, or twig, call out "Change."

5. When someone calls out "Change," the whole group stops so the person who called out can make a note on his or her Results Table. Use tally marks to show repeated actions.

6. Use the listed changes in the Results Table and add other changes as needed.

7. Make sure not to litter. If you drop something, pick it up.

Results

Environmental Changes You Noticed
Broke a twig
Stepped on a plant
Stepped on a bug
Dropped something
Touched something

Name _____ Date _____

Environmental Changes You Noticed
Splashed water

Conclusions

Answer the questions.

1. Which, if any, of the individual changes would be significant if one person did it only once? Explain.

_____

_____

_____

2. Altogether, how many changes did the class count during the experiment?

_____

3. Which, if any, of the different change categories are significant when a whole group does them a few times? Explain.

_____

_____

_____

4. Since you were not able to walk in the forest without causing changes, do you think people should be forbidden to walk in forests? Explain. _____

_____

_____

 Connection to Physical Science

When walking in a forest, do you think larger people cause more environmental change than smaller people do? Think about the differences in height and foot size.

Name _____ Date _____

 Lesson 9: Background

Earth materials include solid rocks, soils, water, and air. These materials deal with warmth and cold differently.

When the sun shines on soil. . .	When the sun shines on water. . .
it warms just the top of it.	the sun's rays can go deep into the water and spread out.
So soil and sand are warm on the very top, but cooler under the surface.	So the top one or two feet of water is often warmer than the lower depth of water.

Since the surface of the ground does not share the heat with the area below it, the ground on a warm day at the beach usually feels warmer than the water. In addition, it takes more heat to raise the temperature of water than it does to raise the temperature of soil. So the water is warming up more slowly and spreading the warmth out more. On the other hand, since water can hold heat longer than air, the warmer water is the reason that coastal cities often have warmer winters than do inland cities. Coastal cities stay cooler in summer because water takes more heat energy to heat up.

On Earth, we have three types of rock.

Igneous rocks. . .	Sedimentary rocks. . .	Metamorphic rocks. . .
have a crystal structure	have a layered structure	are formed through change in the condition of rocks (note the similarity to the word *metamorphosis*)
are formed when **lava** or **magma** cool and create crystals	are formed from the compacting of plant, animal, and general **sediment** into layers	are created when heat and pressure act on igneous or sedimentary rocks

Natural changes in rocks create the **rock cycle**. Each of the three types of rock can change into any of the other two types.

 Connection to Life Science

Look in books, magazines, encyclopedias, or on the Internet to find animals that rely on rocks and/or dirt for their life routines. Create a poster showcasing one of the animals and its use of rocks and/or dirt.

Name _____ Date _____

Experiment 1: Holding Heat

Purpose Water, air, and soil warm and cool at different rates. You will explore these rates in this experiment.

Procedure

1. Place the two cups and two glasses in a refrigerator.

2. Set the timer for 10 minutes.

3. Take the two plastic cups out of the refrigerator and reset the timer for 5 minutes.

4. Measure the temperature of the soil and water in the plastic cups. Record the temperatures in the Results Table columns under #1.

5. Place one plastic cup on the flat surface in the sun and set a timer for 15 minutes.

6. Place the other plastic cup on the flat surface in the sun and set the other timer for 15 minutes.

7. When the first timer rings, take the two glasses out of the refrigerator.

8. Holding one of the glasses in each hand, feel if there is a temperature difference. Record your observation in the Results Table column under #2.

9. When the second timer rings, again measure the temperature of the soil and water in the plastic cups.

10. Record the temperatures in the Results Table columns under #3.

Materials

A plastic disposable cup filled with soil that is at room temperature

A plastic disposable cup filled with water that is at room temperature

A drinking glass filled with soil that is at room temperature

An empty drinking glass

2 timers

Refrigerator

2 thermometers

Counter or other flat surface in sunlight

Results

#1		#2	#3	
Water temperature	Soil temperature	Does one of the glasses feel warmer than the other? _____ If so, which one?	Water temperature	Soil temperature

Practical Science 3–4, SV 9781419099182

Conclusions

Answer the questions.

1. Does soil or water cool down faster? How do you know?

_____

_____

2. Does soil or air cool down faster? How do you know?

_____

_____

3. Does air or water cool down faster? How do you know?

_____

_____

4. Does soil or water heat up faster? How do you know?

_____

_____

Connection to Life Science

Research to find some animals that take advantage of the fact that, in a cold climate, the soil is warmer than the air in the winter.

Name _____ Date _____

Experiment 2: Sorting Rocks

Purpose   There are three main types of rocks: igneous, metamorphic, and sedimentary. You can sort rocks by these types as well as by other traits. In this experiment, you will sort rocks in different ways.

Materials
For each group of 2–4 students:
A collection of at least 20 different
    types and sizes of rocks (At least
    2 igneous, 2 metamorphic, and
    2 sedimentary)
3 magnifying glasses
Internet access

Procedure

1. Sort the rocks into the different sizes listed in the first column of the Results Table.

2. Write the number of each rock size in the Results Table.

3. Sort the rocks into the different colors listed in the second column of the Results Table. Use the magnifying glasses as needed.

4. Write the number of each rock color in the Results Table.

5. Sort the rocks into the different shapes listed in the third column of the Results Table. Use the magnifying glasses as needed.

6. Write the number of each rock shape in the Results Table.

7. Sort the rocks into the different edges listed in the fourth column of the Results Table. Use the magnifying glasses as needed.

8. Write the number of each kind of rock edge in the Results Table.

9. Use the Internet to find a Web site that shows pictures of igneous, sedimentary, and metamorphic rocks. Use the pictures to help you sort the rocks into the final column. Use the magnifying glasses as needed.

10. Write the number of each rock type in the Results Table.

11. Keep your last sort in place as you answer the Conclusions questions.

Name _____ Date _____

Results

Size	Color	Shape	Edges	Rock Type
Small	White/Beige	Round	Smooth	Igneous
Medium	Tan/Brown	Long and thin	Sharp	Sedimentary
Large	Reddish	Short and fat	None	Metamorphic
	Gray/Black	Other	Other	
	Other			

Conclusions

Write the answers.

1. List one feature of igneous rocks. _____

2. List one feature of sedimentary rocks. _____

3. List one feature of metamorphic rocks. _____

 Connection to Physical Science

You can often identify rocks by marks they can make on paper. Rocks that make similar marks are usually made of similar minerals. Test the rocks you have to see if any of them make marks on paper. Group together any that make similar marks. Find out what the rocks might have in common that causes them to make such marks.

Experiment 3: Exploring Uses of Water, Dirt, and Rock

Purpose Since water, dirt, and rocks are natural Earth materials, humans naturally use these materials in many ways. In this experiment, you will explore ways that water, dirt, and rocks are used in your area.

Materials
Adult helper

Mapped-out walking area that is about 1 mile long and includes varied uses of water, dirt, and rock

Pencil

Notebook or clipboard to use as a writing surface during walk

Procedure

1. Take a walk with the adult helper, following the area mapped out. Be sure to stay with your group.

2. While walking, look for ways humans have used water, dirt, and rocks.

3. Each time you find an example, stop and describe it on your Results Table.

4. Only note each example once. For example, if you see rock used for the walls of a building on Clark Street and later another one on Cherry Street, only record the one on Clark Street.

Results

Uses for Rock	Uses for Dirt	Uses for Water

Name _____   Date _____

Uses for Rock	Uses for Dirt	Uses for Water

Conclusions

Complete these sentences.

1. Based on what I saw on the walk, people mostly use rock for

   _____.

2. Based on what I saw on the walk, people mostly use water for

   _____.

3. Based on what I saw on the walk, people mostly use dirt for

   _____.

Circle the word that best completes the sentence.

4. On the walk, I did not go a whole (foot, yard, block, mile) without seeing dirt, rock, and/or water in use.

Connection to Life Science

Make a poster showing how some animals use rocks, water, and dirt in their daily lives.

Lesson 10: Background

Fossils provide evidence about the history of life on Earth. Most fossils are very small pieces of the remains of plants and animals. Larger fossils are usually the remains of animals with shells since the hardness of the shells makes these animals easier to preserve.

Some rocks, such as **chalk**, are made up almost completely of fossils. Fossils are not found in igneous rocks since they are not part of the **spontaneous eruptions** of hot magma and lava. Fossils are also not found in metamorphic rock since they do not survive the pressure and heat. Rather, fossils are found in the layers of sedimentary rock.

Scientists use fossils for "relative dating." This means that by comparing the location of like-animal fossils, scientists can determine the age of different layers of rock. Fossils found in the lowest, or deepest, rock represent the oldest forms of life on Earth. Fossils found in higher layers of rock represent animals from later times. When similar fossils are found in rock layers in different parts of the world, scientists assume that these rock layers were created at the same time.

Scientists use fossils to construct realistic exhibits showing whole **ecosystems** from ancient times. This process begins with an understanding of the individual plants and animals that resulted in the fossils they have found. This reconstruction is difficult since most fossils provide only a small part of the original plant or animal. For example, when a fossil shows a small fernlike image, it doesn't show how the leaves attach to the stem nor if the original plant was a small plant, a bush, or a tree. Accurately reconstructing plants from fossils is difficult and sometimes impossible. For this reason, when you see recreated scenes in a museum or book, they are actually scientists' best guesses.

Connection to Physical Science

Find out what minerals have to do with fossil formation.

71

Experiment 1: Finding Fossils

Purpose   Body fossils show the shape of an animal or plant or a part of an animal or plant. Trace fossils show evidence of an animal's life, such as footprints. Both body and trace fossils appear in sedimentary rock. In this experiment, you will search through rocks looking for fossils.

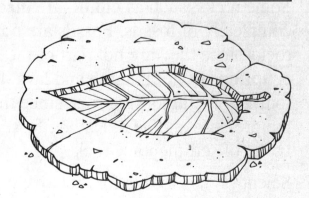

Materials

A collection of rocks, some with trace fossils, some with body fossils, and some with no fossils

Magnifying glass

Procedure

1. Using a magnifying glass, inspect one rock at a time.

2. In the Results Table, draw the first six fossils you find.

3. Circle *Body* or *Trace* in the Results Table to identify each fossil.

Results

First Fossil **Body** **Trace**	Second Fossil **Body** **Trace**	Third Fossil **Body** **Trace**
Fourth Fossil **Body** **Trace**	Fifth Fossil **Body** **Trace**	Sixth Fossil **Body** **Trace**

Conclusions

Answer the questions.

1. What is the most common type of fossil you observed?

_____

_____

_____

2. Was it difficult to decide the type of fossil you observed? Explain.

_____

_____

_____

3. How did the body fossils differ from the trace fossils?

_____

_____

_____

4. Which fossil did you find most interesting? Describe it. Explain your choice.

_____

_____

_____

Connection to Life Science

Make a list of five animals that are likely to be found in fossils and five that are not likely to be found in fossils. Explain your choices.

Experiment 2: Creating Shell Fossils

Purpose   Fossils are created when an animal or plant mixes with sand and other sediment and, over thousands of years, is pressed into sedimentary rock. In this experiment, you will use a shortcut to simulate the creation of a fossil.

Materials

Large saucepan
Wooden mixing spoon
Adult helper
Hot plate
Cutting board
Hammer
For each student:
1 cup clean beach sand (no shells, plants, etc.)
$\frac{1}{2}$ tsp alum
$\frac{1}{4}$ cup cornstarch
$\frac{3}{4}$ cup water
1 seashell

Procedure

1. Combine the sand, alum, cornstarch, and water in the saucepan. Mix thoroughly with the wooden spoon.

2. Have the adult helper cook and stir the mixture on the hot plate over medium heat until the mixture thickens and begins to hold its shape.

3. Have the adult helper pour the mixture onto a cutting board to cool.

4. The mixture will cool very quickly. As soon as it is cool enough to handle, take a handful.

5. Push the shell into the sand clay and form a clay ball around the shell.

6. Let the sand clay dry for a few days.

7. When the sand clay is hard, have the adult helper assist you in tapping the ball with the hammer to crack the ball into two halves to see the "fossil."

Results

Follow the directions.

1. How do the two halves of your fossil ball look? Describe or draw them.

_____

_____

_____

Name _____ Date _____

Conclusions

Complete each sentence.

1. One way that the homemade fossil is like a real fossil is

   _____

   _____.

2. One way that the homemade fossil is NOT like a real fossil is

   _____

   _____.

Circle the correct answer.

3. In this experiment, which part of the natural fossil process does the heat represent?

   A. the crumbling of rock to reveal a fossil

   B. the glue that holds the fossil in place

   C. the pressure and heat that builds up over many years

   D. the part of the animal that is preserved

4. In this experiment, which part of the natural fossil process does the shell represent?

   A. the crumbling of rock to reveal a fossil

   B. the glue that holds the fossil in place

   C. the pressure and heat that builds up over many years

   D. the part of the animal that is preserved

 Connection to Life Science

Choose an animal that often becomes a fossil. Look in books, magazines, encyclopedias, or on the Internet to find out which parts of your chosen animal are typically included in a fossil and which parts are not typically included.

Name _____   Date _____

Experiment 3: Starting with a Fossil

Purpose   Most plant fossils show only a small part of the original plant. Scientists use the small parts to reconstruct whole plants, and in this experiment, you will start with a fossil and reconstruct a whole plant.

Materials
Prehistorical plant research sources with detailed images
Rock with a clear plant fossil
Sheet of white paper
Pencil
Green colored pencil

Procedure

1. Look at your fossil and do research to find a picture of a plant that your fossil could be part of.

2. Place a fossil rubbing in the lower left corner of your paper by placing that corner of your paper over the fossil. Making sure to hold the paper <u>very still</u>, rub back and forth with your pencil lead until the entire outline of the fossil shows on your paper.

3. On the rest of the paper, draw a full picture of a plant that could be the source of the fossil.

4. When you finish drawing, use your green colored pencil to color a part of the plant that could be represented by the fossil. If, for example, your fossil is a single leaf, choose one leaf of your drawing to represent the fossil.

5. At the top of your paper, write the name of the plant you drew.

Results

Answer the questions.

1. What is the name of the plant you drew? _____

2. Where did you find the picture of the plant you drew? _____

_____

Name _____ Date _____

Conclusions

Answer the questions.

1. Why is it important to hold your paper very still while you make a fossil rubbing?

_____

_____

_____

2. Why is it important to use <u>prehistorical</u> plant research sources?

_____

_____

_____

3. Which part of your drawing did you have to guess about since the fossil did not show it?

_____

_____

_____

4. Aside from the plant you chose, did you see other plants that your fossil could have been part of? Explain your answer.

_____

_____

5. How did you decide which plant to use for your drawing?

_____

_____

_____

↻ Connection to Life Science

Find a picture of a fossil from a plant that scientists believe is now an extinct plant. Write a paragraph explaining why the plant might now be extinct.

Name _____   Date _____

 Lesson 11: Background

Water is an important part of life on Earth. Living things need water to stay alive. Think about how many different ways people use water. To name a few examples, people use it to drink, to water plants, to wash themselves and other objects, to cook, and to cool off. Water is a part of people's everyday lives.

About 70% of Earth's surface is covered with water. Water can also be found in Earth's air and underground. Most of Earth's water is salt water. People cannot drink salt water, so they must drink fresh water that comes from rivers, streams, lakes, and groundwater.

Earth's water constantly changes. Its repeated changing is known as the **water cycle**. Water in the cycle can be a solid (ice), liquid (water), or gas (water vapor). Ice can become water or water vapor. Water can become water vapor or ice, and water vapor can become water or ice. The water cycle continually supplies Earth with fresh water. There are three main parts of the cycle:

- **precipitation** (Rain, snow, or sleet falls to Earth and collects in lakes, rivers, oceans, and groundwater.)

- **evaporation** (Water on Earth warms up from the sun's heat, turns into vapor, and goes into the air.)

- **condensation** (Water vapor in the air gets cold, turns into liquid water, and forms clouds.)

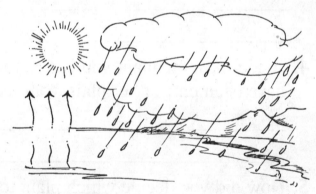

 Connection to Life Science

Find out the meaning of the word *transpiration* and explain how it fits into the water cycle.

Experiment 1: Making a Cloud

Purpose   Clouds form when warm, moist air meets cold, dry air. In this experiment, you will use warm, moist air and cold, dry air to create a cloud.

Materials

For every group:

3 ice cubes

Small metal container (such as a clean tuna can)

Timer

1 sheet of black construction paper

Empty water bottle (.5 L–1 L)

2 cups hot water

Black marker

Procedure

1. Place the ice cubes in the metal container.

2. Set the timer for 1 minute. During this time, wait for the ice cubes to make the metal container cold.

3. Create a backdrop with the black paper up behind the water bottle. This will help you to see a cloud formation in the bottle.

4. Fill the water bottle $\frac{1}{3}$ full of hot water.

5. Place the metal container (with the ice still in it) on top of the bottle.

6. Watch carefully for a cloud to form at the top of the bottle.

7. Use the black marker to draw the bottom of the cloud on the bottle.

Results

Compare the size of your cloud to the size of other students' clouds.

_____

_____

_____

Name _____ Date _____

Conclusions

Circle the correct answer.

1. Which of these choices explains why a cloud forms at the top of the bottle?

    A. Warm, moist air from inside the bottle meets the cold, dry air around the bottom of the container.

    B. Warm, dry air from inside the bottle meets the cold, moist air around the bottom of the container.

    C. Cold, dry air from inside the bottle meets the warm, moist air around the bottom of the container.

2. Even though you cannot see it happening in the bottle, you know that some of the water has—

    A. leaked out.

    B. evaporated.

    C. boiled.

    D. dried up.

Answer the questions.

3. Why does the backdrop make it easier to see the cloud? Explain.

    _____

    _____

    _____

4. Would this experiment have the same result if you dropped the ice cubes into the water instead of putting them in the metal container? Explain.

    _____

    _____

    _____

 Connection to Physical Science

Research to find out how the formation of clouds relates to the water cycle.

Name _____ Date _____

Experiment 2: Removing Salt from Water

Purpose People and plants need fresh water, but most of the water on Earth is salt water. In this experiment, you will discover how the oceans help supply fresh water.

Materials
For every group:
2 cups of salt water
Large mixing bowl
2 cotton swabs
Glass drinking glass
Clinging plastic wrap
Golf ball
Window with sunlight
Pencil
Black marker

Procedure

1. Pour the 2 cups of salt water in the bowl.

2. Dip a cotton swab into the salt water and touch the swab to your tongue to taste the salt water.

3. In the first row of the Results Table, describe how the water tastes.

4. Place the empty glass in the center of the bowl, making sure that the glass is higher than the water level.

5. Stretch plastic wrap over the top of the bowl and seal the edges.

6. Place the golf ball in the center of the plastic wrap so that it draws the plastic wrap downward toward the glass, but without touching the glass.

7. Place the bowl in a sunny window.

8. Wait for 3 or more hours.

9. Remove the plastic wrap.

10. Dip a cotton swab into the water within the glass. Touch the swab to your tongue to taste the water in the glass.

11. In the second row of the Results Table, describe how the water tastes.

12. Place a pencil beside the glass. Use a black marker to draw a line on the pencil to show the level of water in the glass.

Results

Water Choice	What does the water taste like?
Salt water in bowl	
Water in glass	

Conclusions

Circle the correct answer.

1. About how much of the original 2 cups of water were in the glass at the end of the experiment?

   A. all of it

   B. most of it

   C. about half of it

   D. less than half of it

2. In this experiment, the sun caused the water to—

   A. freeze.

   B. melt.

   C. evaporate.

   D. condense.

3. One thing you learn about salt in this experiment is that it does not—

   A. have a taste.

   B. evaporate.

   C. freeze.

   D. belong in water.

Answer the questions.

4. In this experiment, what is the purpose of the golf ball?

   _____

   _____

   _____

5. How does this experiment explain why the oceans are filled with salt water that is constantly evaporating, and why rain is fresh water?

   _____

   _____

   _____

 Connection to Life Science

Think of a substance that sometimes gets into lakes and rivers and is unhealthy for animals. Write a paragraph explaining how the substance gets into natural waters and how to keep it out of the waters.

Name _____ Date _____

Experiment 3: Understanding the Water Cycle

Purpose Water moves through the water cycle and changes form. In this experiment, you will see how water changes form through condensation and evaporation. You will also observe how the sun plays a role in the water cycle.

Materials
1 cup water
2 clear containers
Plastic wrap
Rubber band

Procedure

1. Measure $\frac{1}{2}$ cup water into each container.

2. Cover each container tightly with plastic wrap.

3. Use the rubber band to secure the plastic wrap in place.

4. Place one container in a spot with direct sunlight and place the other container in a shady spot.

5. Observe each container every day for 5 days. Record your observations each day in the Results Table.

Results

Sunny Spot				
Day One	**Day Two**	**Day Three**	**Day Four**	**Day Five**

Shady Spot				
Day One	Day Two	Day Three	Day Four	Day Five

Conclusions

Answer the questions.

1. Which container formed condensation first? _____

2. Where did the water go after it condensed on the plastic wrap? What does this represent in the water cycle?

_____

_____

_____

3. Which container, if any, had its water evaporate first? _____

4. What does this experiment tell you about how the sun affects the water cycle?

_____

_____

Connection to Physical Science

It is a natural change when water changes back and forth from solid to liquid to gas. This change is natural since the substance is still chemically water no matter which stage it is in and can continually change back to other states. Some substances change in ways that do not allow them to change back. For example, heat causes bread dough to change into bread, and bread dough cannot change back into bread. This change is called a chemical change. Make a list of two natural changes (other than water changing) and two chemical changes (other than bread dough changing).

Name _____ Date _____

 Lesson 12: Background

Three natural occurrences that can cause problems for humans are icebergs, landslides, and erosion. All three involve a powerful Earth force: water.

Icebergs are large pieces of frozen, freshwater ice. These pieces of ice, which are floating in open water, break off from larger areas of ice. Since much or all of an iceberg is below the water, they create a serious problem for ships in the open ocean. You have probably heard of the *Titanic*. It was a ship that sank in 1912 because it ran into an iceberg that the ship staff did not see. After this tragedy, new systems were created to detect unseen icebergs.

Landslides take place in steep areas. They are a type of **natural disaster** where the land moves into a sloping position rapidly and suddenly. Most landslides are common in higher areas of mountains, and these landslides usually cause no problems for people since they are uninhabited areas. But, landslides also take place in lower mountains and hilly areas where people do live. These landslides often destroy homes, roads, planned plant growth, and can even result in human injury or death.

The oceans, seas, and rivers in the world are constantly wearing away the land that they border or flow through. For example, huge **canyons** are created from thousands of years of a river flowing through and constantly taking little pieces of rock and dirt with it. Also oceans bump up against beaches and slowly eat away at them. This slow, but ongoing, eating away at land by water is called **erosion**.

 Connection to Physical Science

Create a poster showing why water is sometimes called H_2O.

Experiment 1: Understanding Icebergs

Purpose Icebergs are pieces of ice that break off and float in open water. In this experiment, you will explore the effect of melting icebergs.

Procedure

1. Fill your glass with ice. Use as much ice as possible, making sure that no ice cubes stick up past the top rim of the glass.

2. Add water to the glass, filling it right up to the rim.

3. Place the glass inside the cereal bowl in case any water overflows while the ice melts.

4. Let the glass sit until the ice melts.

5. Observe what happens as the ice melts.

Results

Answer the questions.

1. Did any water overflow into the bowl? _____

2. Is the glass still full to the rim? _____

Conclusions

Circle the correct answer.

1. This experiment shows that—

   A. the ice took up more space than the water it turned into.

   B. the water the ice turned into took up more space than the ice did.

   C. the ice and the water the ice turned into took up the same amount of space.

   D. most of the water evaporated before the ice melted.

2. If an iceberg was barely visible on the top of a lake and then the iceberg melted, what would be the effect on the surrounding lake?

   A. The shoreline of the lake would show the lake is fuller.

   B. The shoreline of the lake would show the lake is emptier.

   C. The shoreline of the lake would show the lake is the same fullness.

   D. The entire lake would dry up.

3. If an iceberg showed a huge piece of ice floating on top of a lake and then it melted, what would be the effect on the surrounding lake?

A. If anything, the shoreline of the lake would show the lake is fuller.

B. If anything, the shoreline of the lake would show the lake is emptier.

C. If anything, the shoreline of the lake would show the lake is the same fullness.

D. If anything, the entire lake would dry up.

Answer the question.

4. How would the results of this experiment have been different if the ice had been piled high above the rim before the water was added?

_____

_____

 Connection to Life Science

Look to find changes that icebergs cause in water ecosystems. Create a poster demonstrating one of the changes you find.

Name _____ Date _____

Experiment 2: Exploring Landslides

Purpose Landslides happen when the ground on a hill gets more water than it can handle. In this experiment, you will explore circumstances that cause landslides.

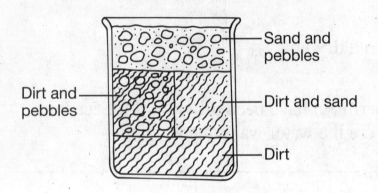

Materials

For each team of 2–4 students:

1 cake pan

1 gallon of dirt

$\frac{1}{2}$ gallon of pebbles

1 gallon of sand

2 gallons of water

3 small plastic toy houses, such as from a board game

5 books, each about 2 inches thick

Large measuring cup

Procedure

1. Cover the bottom of the cake pan with about 1 inch of dirt, pebbles, and sand.

2. Layer the dirt, pebbles, and sand out as shown in the diagram and dampen the dirt with water to help hold it in place.

3. Place the houses on the "land" you have created.

4. Place one end of the cake pan on one of the books.

5. Pour water into the large measuring cup. Gently and slowly pour water into the pan at the end that is up in the air.

6. Stop pouring when a "landslide" occurs. In other words, stop when houses, dirt, rocks, and/or sand let loose from the bottom of the pan.

7. Record the amount of water you used in the Results Table.

8. Remove the water and dirt from the pan. Refill the measuring cup with water.

9. Repeat Steps 1–8, but with three books instead of one.

10. Repeat Steps 1–8, but with five books instead of three.

Name _____ Date _____

Results

One-Book Results		Three-Book Results		Five-Book Results	
Describe the area of the pan where the landslide took place.	How much water did you pour before the landslide happened?	Describe the area of the pan where the landslide took place.	How much water did you pour before the landslide happened?	Describe the area of the pan where the landslide took place.	How much water did you pour before the landslide happened?

Conclusions

Answer the questions.

1. Based on your results, what effect does steepness of land have on landslides?

_____

_____

_____

2. In this experiment, do you think the rate at which you pour the water makes a difference? Explain.

_____

_____

_____

Circle the best answer.

3. Based on your results, which type of ground cover is most likely to be involved in a landslide?

    sand and pebbles   dirt and pebbles   dirt and sand   dirt

4. If you were going to build a house on a hill, which type of land cover would you choose in hopes of preventing a landslide?

    sand and pebbles   dirt and pebbles   dirt and sand   dirt

 **Connection to Physical Science**

Research the meaning of *gravity*. Explain what gravity has to do with this experiment.

      Practical Science 3–4, SV 9781419099182

Experiment 3: Creating Erosion

Purpose Erosion causes land to flow into rivers, oceans, and other bodies of water. In this experiment, you will explore causes of erosion in a beach environment.

Materials

For each team of 2–4 students:
Cake pan
3 gallons of soil
Measuring cup
Sand bucket
Cereal bowl
2-quart pitcher
2 gallons of water
4 straws
Digital timer

Procedure

1. Pack soil firmly in the sand bucket. Quickly flip the bucket so the contents form a tall structure of soil in one end of the cake pan.

2. Pack soil firmly in the cereal bowl. Quickly flip the bowl to form a low structure in one end of the cake pan.

3. Sprinkle 1 cup of loose soil around the two molded structures.

4. Using the pitcher, pour 2 cups of water down the center-top of both of the structures.

5. Note any changes you see in each of the #1 boxes in the Results Table.

6. Use the straws to blow air on the soil structures for 30 seconds. Blow downward so as not to blow soil outside of the pan.

7. Note any changes you see in each of the #2 boxes in the Results Table.

8. For 30 seconds, slosh the water in the pan from side to side. Move it as much as you can without sloshing water out of the pan. Use the digital timer.

9. Note any changes you see in the #3 box in the Results Table.

10. For 60 seconds, again slosh the water in the pan from side to side. Move it as much as you can without sloshing water out of the pan. Use the digital timer.

11. Note any changes you see in the #4 box in the Results Table.

Name _____ Date _____

Results

#1 Does the tall structure look different than before you poured the water? Explain.	#1 Does the short structure look different than before you poured the water? Explain.	#2 Does the tall structure look different than before you blew through the straws? Explain.	#2 Does the short structure look different than before you blew through the straws? Explain.	#3 What, if any, changes did you see after sloshing the water for 30 seconds? Explain.	#4 What, if any, changes did you see after sloshing the water for 60 more seconds? Explain.

Conclusions

Circle the word or words that best complete the sentences.

1. Blowing through the straws in this experiment represents _____ in actual erosion.

   wind   rain   people

2. Pouring the water on top of the structures represents _____ in actual erosion.

   a gentle rain   a windy day   very large waves

3. Sloshing water from side to side represents _____ in actual erosion.

   very heavy rain   gentle but constant waves   people running and playing

Answer the question.

4. Of the actions, which caused the most erosion?

   pouring   blowing   sloshing

 Connection to Physical Science

Waves have different wavelengths and wave frequencies. At a given speed, the more waves there are in a set amount of time, the shorter the wavelength, and the more energy the wave has. Which is likely to cause more erosion, waves with higher or lower frequency?

Name _____   Date _____

Lab Sheet

Experiment: _____

Purpose:
Observations:
Results:
Conclusions:

Glossary

air molecules   (p. 14) the smallest pieces of air

attract   (p. 21) to pull towards

bone conduction   (p. 14) the passing of sound vibrations through the head bones to the inner ear without passing through the outer ear

canyon   (p. 85) deep valley, often with rocky sides and a river or stream flowing through it

chalk   (p. 71) a soft, white powdery limestone formed mostly out of fossils

charge   (p. 28) a positive or negative characteristic of a particle that exerts an electrical force on other charged particles

circuit   (p. 28) a path through which electric current can flow

condensation   (p. 78) the process of changing from gas to liquid

conductor   (p. 7) a material that lets sound travel through it

contract   (p. 43) to move muscles by shortening and lengthening

crop residue   (p. 57) roots, stems, and leaves of crops remaining after the crop has been harvested

crop rotation   (p. 57) to plant different crops in a field to help keep the soil healthy

decibels   (p. 7) a unit for measuring the loudness of sound

digestive system   (p. 43) the system that makes food useful to the body

eardrum   (p. 7) a membrane between the outer ear and the middle ear

Earth materials   (p. 64) the solids, liquids, and gases (matter) that make up Earth

ecosystem   (p. 71) a community of plants and animals and their environment

electric current   (p. 28) flow of electricity through a conductor

electromagnet   (p. 28) a magnet that is only magnetized when electric current flows through it

environment   (p. 57) the surroundings of a plant or animal

erosion   (p. 85) the slow and ongoing moving away of land by water, wind, or gravity

evaporation   (p. 78) the process of changing from liquid to gas

force   (p. 7) a push or a pull

fossil   (p. 71) a hardened part of an animal or trace of an animal (such as a footprint) found in rocks

friction   (p. 28) resistance

iceberg   (p. 85) large piece of ice that is floating in open water

igneous rock   (p. 64) rock that forms from lava or magma

inner ear   (p. 7) the part of the ear that transfers sound from the middle ear to the brain by way of the auditory nerve

integumentary system   (p. 43) the body system that includes skin, hair, nails, and sweat glands

landslide   (p. 85) falling or sliding of soil and/or rock down a steep slope

large intestine   (p. 43) the last part of the digestive system before solid waste leaves the body

lava   (p. 64) melted rock from a volcano

liquid   (p. 14) type of matter that flows freely; not solid or gas

maggots   (p. 50) fly eggs that are often laid on rotting food and help the food to rot

magma   (p. 64) melted rock inside the earth

magnet   (p. 21) an object that attracts iron or steel

magnetic   (p. 21) being able to attract iron or steel

Practical Science 3–4, SV 9781419099182

magnetism   (p. 21) power to attract; attraction for iron and steel

metamorphic rock   (p. 64) rock formed by putting heat and pressure on igneous and metamorphic rock

middle ear   (p. 7) the part of the ear that transfers sound from the outer ear to the inner ear

mirage   (p. 35) something seen in the distance that is not actually there; often an optical illusion in a desert

molecule   (p. 7) the smallest particle of a substance

muscle   (p. 35) tissues that contract, providing movement

natural disaster   (p. 85) a natural phenomenon such as a hurricane, tornado, or avalanche that causes damage to Earth

nerve impulses   (p. 7) messages sent through the body by the nervous system

nutrient   (p. 43) part of food that is useful to the body

omnivores   (p. 50) animals that eat both plants and animals

optical illusions   (p. 35) eye tricks; things that are not necessarily what they look like

organism   (p. 57) a living thing

outer ear   (p. 7) the visible part of the ear that collects sounds

permanent magnet   (p. 28) magnet that always attracts steel or iron

poles   (p. 21) the opposite ends of magnets that have positive and negative attractions

precipitation   (p. 78) rain, snow, or sleet

repel   (p. 28) to resist

rock cycle   (p. 64) process by which rock forms and changes into other kinds of rock

saliva   (p. 43) a watery fluid in the mouth that is part of the digestive system and helps break food down

sediment   (p. 64) solid matter such as sand that is deposited by the wind, water, and ice

sedimentary rock   (p. 64) rock formed by compacting plants, animals, and sediment into layers

small intestine   (p. 43) the part of the digestive system between the stomach and the large intestine

soil erosion   (p. 57) the process by which soil is carried away by water

solids   (p. 14) type of matter with a definite shape; not gas or liquid

sound amplification   (p. 7) methods of making noises louder and more easily heard

soundproofing   (p. 7) methods of blocking noise

sound waves   (p. 7) vibrations that travel through air and can be heard or detected

spontaneous eruptions   (p. 71) explosions without warning

static electricity   (p. 28) a buildup of electric charge caused by friction

strip cropping   (p. 57) to plant sections of two or more crops within one field in an effort to stop erosion

structures   (p. 50) any identifiable part of an organism

sweat glands   (p. 43) structures through which excess water leaves the body

taste buds   (p. 43) structures on the tongue that allow people to taste foods

temporary magnets   (p. 28) magnet that can be magnetized, but is not always magnetized

vibration   (p. 7) motion in a rhythm or pattern

water cycle   (p. 78) path that water follows as it moves from the air to the ground and back to the air over and over again

Practical Science 3–4, SV 9781419099182

Answer Key

This answer key includes answers to the Conclusions only. It is important to note that the students' answers may vary, depending on their experiment results. Science experiments are not always predictable. Use your best judgment when checking answers.

Lesson 1 Experiment 1
Knowing What You Hear, p. 9
1. Answers will vary but should include that students could have used their previous knowledge about noises that different things make.
2.–3. Answers will vary.

Lesson 1 Experiment 2
Identifying Loud and Soft, p. 11
1. Answers will vary.
2. Answers will vary but will likely suggest using carpet pads.
3. Yes, some materials, such as solids, absorb sound better than others. Their molecules are closer together, making it easier for sound to move from one molecule to another.

Lesson 1 Experiment 3
Hearing Through Things, p. 13
1. Answers will vary.
2. Answers will vary depending on the specific items that are used, but the pillow is likely to block more sound than the cutting board.
3. Answers will vary depending on the specific items that are used, but the bag of water is not likely to block as much sound as the book.

Lesson 2 Experiment 1
Looking at Sound, p. 16
1. Students heard the sound.
2. The rice moved.
3. The rice slowly slowed down before it stopped moving.

Lesson 2 Experiment 2
Feeling Sound, p. 18
1. Answers will vary but might include the idea that louder noises result in stronger vibrations.
2. Answers will vary but might logically target the one-hour timer since its vibrations are probably not strong enough to feel.
3. Answers will vary but might suggest that it is sometimes hard to both make a noise and feel the sound vibrations.
4. Answers will vary but might include the idea that the softest sound resulted in a vibration that could not be felt.

Lesson 2 Experiment 3
Conducting Sound, p. 20
1. Answers will vary.
2. Sound travels better through a solid. The molecules are closer together, so

the sound can bounce from one to another more easily.

Lesson 3 Experiment 1
Exploring Magnets, p. 23
1. A and C   2. C and D
3. Answers will vary but should include items made of steel or stainless steel.

Lesson 3 Experiment 2
Making a Magnet, p. 25
1. Answers will vary but should suggest that the paper clip was only magnetized for a little while. This was temporary.
2. The large magnet is considered to be a temporary magnet because it was only magnetized for a temporary amount of time.
3. B

Lesson 3 Experiment 3
Magnet Races, p. 26
1. Answers will vary but might include that it was difficult to hold the paper still and that it was difficult to maintain contact with the paper clip.
2. It is clear that a magnet definitely attracts through paper.

Lesson 4 Experiment 1
Magnetizing Balloons, p. 30
1. rubbing a balloon on your hair, rubbing a balloon on your clothes
2. Answers will vary but are likely to include the observation that, since the balloons started falling off while the rice was being prepared, the static electricity did not last very long.
3. B   4. C

Lesson 4 Experiment 2
Creating a Magnetic Field, p. 32
1. round   2. C   3. A   4. B

Lesson 4 Experiment 3
Constructing a Circuit, p. 34
1. open circuit
2. closed circuit
3. Answers may vary but should include that when the tongue touched the coins a circuit was created. This caused an electric current to flow.
4. No, because there would not be a circuit.

Lesson 5 Experiment 1
Testing Finger Strength, p. 37
1. A   2. middle finger
3. Answers may vary.

Lesson 5 Experiment 2
Using Tired Eyes, p. 39
1. Answers will vary but are likely to indicate that the shape did move up and down a little bit and that one or both of the stars sometimes faded in and out.
2. white   3. blue   4. purple

Lesson 5 Experiment 3
Aiming with One Eye, pp. 40–41
1.–3. Answers will vary based on individual results.
4. Answers will vary based on individual results but should involve the same eye as in the answer to question 1.

Lesson 6 Experiment 1
Moving Bananas Through, p. 45
1. Answers may vary based on individual results.
2. The banana represents food moving through the digestive system. Some foods are absorbed by the body, and some are left as waste.
3. D

Lesson 6 Experiment 2
Using Taste Buds, p. 47
1. Answers might vary but will most likely be as follows going clockwise from the center back: coffee, lemon juice, salt water, sugar water, salt water, lemon juice.
2. Answers will vary, but students are likely to indicate that they had some trouble deciding on some of the strongest taste areas.
3. Since the front of the tongue is where the sweet taste buds are located, it makes sense that licking an ice-cream cone with the front of the tongue would enhance the sweet taste of the ice cream.
4. People who direct the coffee to the center-back area are putting the coffee on the area of the tongue that most strongly senses bitter tastes. Since coffee has a bitter taste, people who choose this method of drinking coffee most likely prefer the strong taste of coffee.

Lesson 6 Experiment 3
Confusing Your Skin, pp. 48–49
1. The room temperature water did not feel the same to both hands. It felt warm on the cold hand and cool on the hot hand.
2. The senses of warm and cool in the room temperature would probably not have been as strong since the hands would not have had enough time to adjust to the extreme temperatures.
3. B   4. B

Lesson 7 Experiment 1
Growing Plants Without Dirt, p. 52
1. Answers may vary.
2. Answers may vary but will most likely be a root.
3. Answers may vary but are likely to include the idea that the light helped the plants grow and that the plants grew in the direction of the light.

Practical Science 3–4, SV 9781419099182

Lesson 7 Experiment 2
Planting Groceries, p. 54
1. Answers will vary.
2.–4. Answers will depend on specific plantings.

Lesson 7 Experiment 3
Watching Meat Spoil, p. 56
1. Answers will vary, but it was likely only a few days before the maggots appeared.
2. Answers will vary. The meat probably smelled bad before the maggots appeared.
3. Since the flies could not get to the meat in two of the jars, there are no maggots in those two jars.
4. It is clear that meat will spoil with and without maggots since all three meat samples spoiled.
5. It is important to put the jars in a cage since the cage is being left outside and animals would likely eat the meat if they could get to it.

Lesson 8 Experiment 1
Holding Soil, p. 59
1. Since it takes a little while for roots to grow through the soil and wrap around soil particles, a newly planted plant would most likely not hold onto nearly as much soil.
2. Farmers' fields are most safe from erosion when the crops have been growing for a little while and have a hold on the soil. Farmers' fields are least safe from erosion when there are no plants in them at all.
3. A   4. C

Lesson 8 Experiment 2
Digging a Tunnel, p. 61
1.–3. Answers will vary.
4. Answers will vary but will likely suggest that it will make the soil wet and help living things grow.

Lesson 8 Experiment 3
Changing the Environment by Walking, p. 63
1. Answers could vary, but unless someone creates a rather serious environmental change, it is logical to assume that no individual change would be very significant.
2. Answers will vary.
3. Answers will vary but would logically indicate that all changes are significant when enacted many times.
4. No, people should not be forbidden to walk in forests. People are part of the environment, and as such, will logically make some changes in it. However, people should conduct themselves with a sense of responsibility.

Lesson 9 Experiment 1
Holding Heat, p. 66
1. Soil cools down faster than water since, coming out of the refrigerator, the soil is at a lower temperature than the water.

2. Air cools down faster than soil since, coming out of the refrigerator, the soil-filled glass felt warmer.
3. Air cools down faster than water since air cools faster than soil and soil cools faster than water.
4. Soil heats up faster than water since, after being in the sun for 15 minutes, the soil was at a higher temperature.

Lesson 9 Experiment 2
Sorting Rocks, p. 68
1. Answers will vary but might include a color statement.
2. Answers will vary but might include a reference to the obvious layers.
3. Answers will vary but might include a reference to a similarity to igneous or sedimentary rock from which it was formed.

Lesson 9 Experiment 3
Exploring Uses of Water, Dirt, and Rock, p. 70
1.–3. Answers will vary based on what students saw on walk.
4. block (most likely answer)

Lesson 10 Experiment 1
Finding Fossils, p. 73
1.–3. Answers may vary based on individual results.
4. Answers will vary based on each student's opinion.

Lesson 10 Experiment 2
Creating Shell Fossils, p. 75
1. Answers will vary but might include the idea that one half of the sand clay shows an impression of the shell while the other half holds the preserved shell.
2. Answers will vary but might include the idea that a real fossil is not created in a day.
3. C   4. D

Lesson 10 Experiment 3
Starting with a Fossil, p. 77
1. If you move your paper while you are making your rubbing, your fossil imprint will be blurred, harder to see, and harder to match up to a plant in the reference sources.
2. Since fossils are made from plants that lived thousands of years ago, those same plants might not be growing today.
3.–4. Answers will vary based on each student's individual fossil.
5. Answers will vary.

Lesson 11 Experiment 1
Making a Cloud, p. 80
1. A
2. B
3. The cloud has a slight white coloration, and the contrast with the black paper makes it easier to see the white.

4. No, the experiment would not have the same result if you put the ice cubes directly in the water because they would then not help to create the dry, cold air. Further, there would not be two distinctly different areas of air that could meet.

Lesson 11 Experiment 2
Removing Salt from Water, p. 82
1. D   2. C   3. B
4. The golf ball causes the plastic wrap to dip toward the glass, which causes the water that forms on the plastic wrap to drip into the glass.
5. When ocean water evaporates, the salt stays behind, so the water that goes into the air is fresh water.

Lesson 11 Experiment 3
Understanding the Water Cycle, p. 84
1. Answers may vary but will likely be the container in the sunny spot.
2. Answers may vary, but a probable answer is that the water dropped down onto the bottom of the cup. This represents precipitation.
3. Answers may vary but will likely be the container in the sunny spot.
4. The sun plays an important role in the water cycle. When a body of water is in direct sunlight, it will evaporate more quickly than a body of water that is not in direct sunlight.

Lesson 12 Experiment 1
Understanding Icebergs, pp. 86–87
1. A   2. B   3. A
4. The water would have overflowed into the bowl.

Lesson 12 Experiment 2
Exploring Landslides, p. 89
1. Answers will vary but should most likely include an indication that the steeper the land, the less water is needed to create a landslide.
2. Yes, the rate at which I pour the water makes a difference since a faster pour results in more pressure and less ability for water to spread out across more ground cover. So, a faster pour results in a faster, and possibly more damaging, landslide.
3. Answers will vary.
4. Answers will vary based on specific results but might logically suggest that, since plants will grow in dirt, dirt is the best choice.

Lesson 12 Experiment 3
Creating Erosion, p. 91
1. wind   2. very large waves
3. gentle but constant waves
4. Answers will vary.

Answer Key
Practical Science 3–4, SV 9781419099182